MSP® Survival Guide for Programme Managers

London: TSO

part of Williams Lea

Published by TSO (The Stationery Office), part of Williams Lea and available from:

Online
www.tsoshop.co.uk

Mail, Telephone, Fax & E-mail
TSO
PO Box 29, Norwich, NR3 1GN
Telephone orders/General enquiries: 0333 202 5070
Fax orders: 0333 202 5080
E-mail: customer.services@tso.co.uk
Textphone: 0333 202 5077

TSO@Blackwell and other Accredited Agents

A CIP catalogue record for this book is available from the British Library

A Library of Congress CIP catalogue record has been applied for

Aligned with the 2011 edition of *Managing Successful Programmes*

First published 2016

ISBN 9780113314782

Printed in the United Kingdom for The Stationery Office
Material is FSC certified. Sourced from responsible sources.
P002750238 c4 02/16

Contents

List of figures

List of tables

Foreword

Our world is changing more rapidly than ever before. The myriad simultaneous shifts emerge ever-more frequently, and their magnitude and direction are unpredictable. While geopolitical and socioeconomic volatility is becoming increasingly disruptive, technological advances are even more challenging to the status quo. In this dynamic and complex environment, the shelf life of strategic plans is rapidly shrinking, with plans often being declared obsolete soon after their release. Moreover, the 'unthinkable' is no longer unthinkable, elevating risk management to a whole new level. It is for these reasons that this survival guide for programme managers has been written. By bringing MSP to life, it provides helpful and specific advice on how to prioritize and get the important things done.

Achieving success in our fast-moving world is a growing demand. We must constantly re-invent and transform to keep pace. If not, we face acquisition or irrelevance and collapse. This is as true for governments and nations as for private and public companies. During a speech in 2015, Klaus Schwab, founder of the World Economic Forum said, 'In the new world, it is not the big fish which eats the small fish. It is the fast fish which eats the slow fish.' The re-invention and transformational processes often require major capital investments with operating cost considerations. Time is always among the critical factors. Transformational major programmes often include arrays of interdependent projects in multiple locations. These are complex undertakings fraught with risks and challenges – but with these challenges come opportunities for major positive impact. The bigger, more iconic and more difficult the challenge, the more valuable the programme manager becomes.

Abraham Lincoln, the 16th president of the United States, is famously quoted as having said, 'Give me six hours to chop down a tree and I will spend the first four sharpening the axe.' Programme management starts with a deep understanding of the desired outcomes to establish why a given programme is required. With this understanding, the programme manager becomes a strategic partner to the client. Only then can they organize the programme, design the key performance indicators, and define the individual projects that will deliver the required outcomes.

The mental discipline of programme management can be applied to projects as ambitious as building super-tall structures, organizing major global events or even colonizing Mars, or as small-scale as managing your child's rugby team. Whatever the initiative, this guide will provide the step-by-step guidance on the processes, tools and templates to help you successfully manage any programme, and to not only survive but thrive in this volatile, uncertain, complex and wondrous world of opportunity in which we live.

Julio Maggi
Global Director Program Management, Arcadis

Preface

Your career in project management has been going well: not only have you had success with individual projects but you have also been effective in managing groups of projects in your part of the business and have become adept at spinning plates.

Then you get the call. You have been offered the chance as a programme manager; you are going to take it but you know in your heart that this is going to be different from some of your big projects. You have done your MSP course, so you know the theory; you may even be known as an 'MSP practitioner', but now is the moment of truth. You are about to start work on your programme and you realize that the tools and techniques that you have used for project management are not necessarily going to scale up, and applying the concepts in practice is different from learning the theory.

This is when you reach for your survival guide. You will be faced with many dilemmas that will be unique to your organization and will test your commitment and beliefs. We can't provide a formula for this, but we have tried to provide a guide that is based on our experience of working with programmes over the last 20 years. The advice is built around MSP; there are other approaches to programme management but the principles of good programme leadership and the general principles of programme management are universal, so if you are using a different method, it should work equally as well for you.

We have written this guide without the shackles of formality which were applied to the development of the MSP framework itself, and we have focused on the things that will make a difference to you. So, armed with this advice, we think that it's time to drop the chief executive an email and say that you are up for the challenge!

Acknowledgements

ABOUT THE AUTHORS

The authors, Rod Sowden and Geof Leigh, have worked closely together on numerous assignments, and are able to draw on a wealth of experience in programme management. This guide marks a culmination in their collaboration.

Rod Sowden

Rod Sowden of Aspire Europe Ltd is lead author of *Managing Successful Programmes* (MSP) and co-lead author of the latest version of P3M3®. He was a pioneer of the use of MSP at the BBC before he founded Aspire Europe in 2004, a company dedicated to improving organizations' transformational programme performance.

Rod has been a passionate thought leader on MSP for more than 15 years and the work of Aspire Europe is universally recognized. He has extensive experience in improving programme management performance, and is active in leading, assuring and rescuing programmes. For more information on Aspire Europe, visit www.aspireeurope.com

Geof Leigh

Geof Leigh was one of the authors of MSP in 2007 and 2011, and wrote the programme management maturity model for the latest version of P3M3. He has also contributed to other well-known books, including the *Gower Handbook of Programme Management* (2006). With more than 30 years' management experience involving portfolios, programmes and projects, Geof has a passion for helping organizations to successfully manage change. He is a lead trainer, examiner and registered consultant for MSP, and now leads the Aspire Assess services within Aspire Europe.

REVIEWERS

The authors and publisher would like to express grateful thanks for the valuable comments, ideas and suggestions received from the following reviewers: Les Allen, Plymouth City Council; Sarah Barnes, HMG; Nick Carter, Aspire Europe Ltd; Jon Childs, Sheffield Hallam University; Toni Frascini, Sheffield Hallam University; Anne Gibb, AGBA; Lyn Hicks, Exeter City Council; Keith Hull, DVLA; Liz Pattison, Arup; John Power, Department for Energy and Climate Change; John Reading, Teradata; Zoe Sibeko, Sheffield Hallam University; Alison Smith, Met Office, UK; Emma Sparkes, AC Nielsen.

Thanks are also due to the Aspire Europe team who provided essential support, namely Tom Farrow, Ellie Hudson, Sam Jenkins, Claire Rookes, Alice Sowden and Alan Summerfield.

The Survival Guide series

This survival guide is part of a series that has been written for people with key roles in a programme. Each title provides specific, practical advice on how to be effective in a way that the more formal MSP manual (*Managing Successful Programmes*) cannot.

MSP is one of the most widely adopted frameworks for programme management, helping to ensure the successful delivery of transformational change. For a comprehensive understanding of the key roles in MSP, you should also read:

- *MSP Survival Guide for Business Change Managers* for larger sections on benefits management, stakeholder engagement and communication, risk management and blueprinting.
- *MSP Survival Guide for Senior Responsible Owners* which has specific guidance for those people leading the programme and how they should interact with you.

AN MSP GUIDE FOR PROGRAMME MANAGERS

There are many reasons why programmes fail, but failure to grasp the scale of the change being delivered and the inexperience of the programme teams are often contributing factors.

MSP Survival Guide for Programme Managers helps to explain what the programme manager needs to do and why, then provides guidance on how to do it using real-life examples. In particular, it focuses on developing and implementing the processes and supporting techniques that are needed to control a programme.

The structure of the guide is as follows:

- Overview (Chapter 1) gives a summary of the key concepts.
- Part 1 (Chapters 2–10) provides the information that you need to know about the governance themes, your role in developing them, and your relationship with the other key members of the programme team.
- Part 2 (Chapters 11–17) describes the iterations through which the programme passes on its journey, and what you must do to guide it to its final destination – the vision.
- Appendix A provides a useful summary of the information baselines.

1 Overview

1 Overview

This chapter provides you with a summary of the key concepts from *Managing Successful Programmes* (MSP) so that you are familiar with the terminology. It can also act as a quick reference for some of the key concepts that you will need to consider at the outset.

MSP isn't the only programme management framework. There is also an approach from an organization called the Project Management Institute (PMI), but it tends to focus on capital programmes such as information technology, engineering and construction. If your programme comes into any of these categories, it would be worth investigating PMI as it has some excellent content.

1.1 WHAT IS PROGRAMME MANAGEMENT?

MSP defines programme management as 'the action of carrying out the coordinated organization, direction and implementation of a dossier of projects and transformational activities (i.e. the programme) to achieve outcomes and realize benefits of strategic importance to the business'.

The programme manager role is primarily about delivering the means to change, whereas the business change manager (BCM) focuses on making the changes operational to realize the benefits.

Programme management aligns three critical organizational elements (see Figure 1.1):

- Corporate strategy
- Delivery mechanisms for change (projects)
- Business as usual and operations environment.

It manages the natural tension that exists between these elements to deliver transformational change that meets the needs of the organization and its stakeholders.

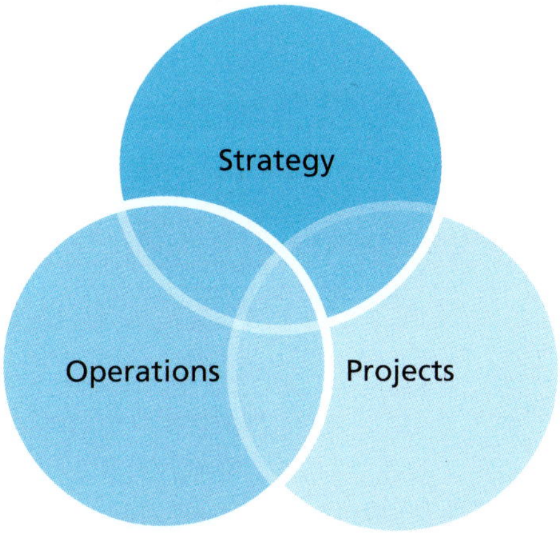

Figure 1.1 Organizational elements of programme management

Programmes can deliver the means to allow business operations to change, but they do not run business operations. It is the senior operational managers who will have to make the changed operations work better than before to realize the benefits for the long term, not the programme.

Within the programme there are three core roles on the programme board. The corporate strategy is represented by the senior responsible owner (SRO), whereas the delivery of the new capability mainly from projects is the responsibility of the programme manager. The definition of the business capability, maintenance of the operational performance and subsequent delivery of benefits are the responsibility of the BCM.

The programme manager must be able to coordinate many projects working with the BCMs, who must have detailed understanding of the business operations and the respect of the operational teams. Working together they will lead people through turbulent times and deliver beneficial change.

1.2 TYPES OF PROGRAMME

There are three distinct types of programme defined in the MSP guide. These are described in Table 1.1.

In reality, most programmes have a mix of these characteristics, but it is helpful to understand the dominant characteristics of a programme as it will help to develop and optimize the priorities and approach. For example, the benefits for a compliance programme may focus on the avoidance of penalties.

Table 1.1 MSP programme types

Programme type	Characteristics
Vision-led	Has come into existence to deliver a clearly defined vision that has been created and sponsored by people at the top of the organization Tends to be top-down in approach, with cross-functional implications for the organization's operations Features entrepreneurial programmes developing new products and services that focus on innovation or strategic opportunity offered by the business environment In the public sector, this could be the translation of political priorities into a programme which will refine and deliver the desired changes
Emergent	Evolves from concurrent, individual projects that have grown within an organization. There is now recognition that coordination of the projects is necessary to deliver the changes and the desired benefits Is transitory, as it becomes a planned programme when its vision, context and direction have been defined and established
Compliance	May also be referred to as a 'must do' programme The organization has no choice but to change as a result of an external event, such as legislative change Benefits may be expressed in terms of compliance, achievement and avoidance of negative implications rather than measurable improvements in performance

Compliance programmes are much more common than is normally recognized. This is because there is a tendency to disguise them as vision-led, which creates more excitement. It is common for change to be forced on the organization by external events. There is no choice, and whether the organization spotted that change early and was first to move, or was last because everyone else already had, is just a matter of timing. Disguising a compliance programme as a vision-led programme can be fraught with danger.

Hints and tips

For you as the programme manager, understanding the type of programme is really important. It is quite often the case that programmes are trumpeted as visionary and the great idea of the chief when in reality this isn't actually the case.

It is very rare to find a genuinely 'blue-sky' vision-led programme where there are no precedents or work going on in the organization. There may be situations where previous work is swept aside by the energy of a new programme, but it is wise not to throw out good work. Consequently, one of the first tasks at the start of many programmes is actually to review what is going on and what can be used in the new initiative.

Whatever type of programme it is, you will be delivering fundamental change of some sort, so you should make sure you are clear about what the drivers for that change are and the source of the energy, as you will need to harness and direct it. If the source of the energy is misunderstood, then you will lose momentum.

Some examples

A large bank had a vision-led programme to change its foreign-currency trading systems. The programme was certainly big, complex and expensive, but after some investigation it transpired that the existing systems were so outdated that they were losing a significant market share. Therefore, the programme was more compliance- than vision-led as the only other real option was to withdraw from currency trading, which wasn't acceptable. The main competitors already had similar systems in place.

A new director general at a large UK public sector organization outlined a vision for the corporation, with 20% fewer staff and leaner and more efficient operations. The organization was already lean and efficient so the vision didn't stand up to scrutiny or dialogue. The reality was that it was another compliance programme as the organization was having central budget cuts imposed on it by government, so it had to comply.

1.3 IMPACTS OF PROGRAMMES

Each type of programme reflects its energy source, and the impacts will also vary. Table 1.2 shows the characteristics of different programme impacts as described in MSP.

The impact of the programmes will vary from sector to sector. Private sector programmes are likely to deliver some sort of specific infrastructure capability, affect internal structure or be trying to effect change in a market or market position. Public sector programmes will do the same but may be trying to effect changes in society and the economy rather than gain market advantage.

Table 1.2 Impacts of programme types

Programme impact	Characteristics
Specification-led	Where the change being delivered is based on the making and delivering of new facilities, the programme will tend to be led by the specification of the outputs required – for example, a major capital construction programme. There will be relatively low levels of ambiguity about what the programme is to deliver but there may be high levels of complexity and risk in the delivery. The scope will be reasonably well defined and adjusted according to circumstances. MSP's approach can be used in this type of programme but may need to be scaled down, as some of its elements may not be required.
Business transformation	Where the change is more focused on transforming the way the organization functions (for example, implementing a new service partnership or moving into a new market) the programme will tend to be vision-led with desired outcomes and associated benefits. There is likely to be ambiguity about the overall implication of the changes; for instance, it may not be known how some parts of the organization will react. The greater the impact on customers and the markets, the greater the levels of ambiguity and risk.
Political and societal	Where the change is focused on improvements in society, the level of predictability will be reduced, as there will be many uncontrollable external factors also at play. For example, a change that aims to improve the early education of pre-school-age children in order to increase their likelihood of making a more meaningful contribution to society when they leave full-time education will not only take time to design and introduce but the implications for the students and the economy will not necessarily be controllable or predictable in the long term. The scope may need to be adjusted as ambiguities are clarified and the changes are delivered in steps (tranches) over a number of years. MSP is highly suitable for programmes with a high level of complexity, ambiguity and risk. The programme management framework of MSP is primarily designed to cater for leading and managing transformational change.

The three impacts are equally relevant to both types of organization. One thing that is for sure is that a programme will deliver some sort of major structural change that will have a lasting effect. Table 1.3 gives some examples.

Not all programmes are quite as spectacular as some of these but hopefully Table 1.3 will help to explain that programme management is applicable to many sectors.

Most programmes will have multiple 'impacts'. This is important for the programme manager as there will be a need to oversee multiple concurrent projects. Some will go well – others will have problems. Some will drift off scope. At some point they will need to deliver the means for coherent organization change. You will need to keep them all in line, speed some up, slow some down and redirect others. The building of a high-speed rail link is a complex engineering challenge that could

Table 1.3 Programme impact examples

Impact	Private sector	Public sector
Specification-led	New distribution network, warehouses, vehicles, ICT etc. (e.g. for a supermarket distributor)	Major new power generation (e.g. Three Gorges Dam project in China)
	New oil exploration platforms (e.g. deep-sea)	New transport infrastructure (e.g. the High Speed 2 (HS2) rail link in the UK)
Business transformation	Merger or acquisition of two large organizations (e.g. UK banks)	Service partner model (e.g. health care provision)
	Adoption of a major new technology (e.g. an enterprise-wide technology)	Deregulation of a sector or market (e.g. banking)
Political and societal	Changing market behaviours (e.g. mobile applications)	Changing the way a market works (e.g. use of non-carbon fuels)
	Creating new customer interfaces and channels (e.g. online purchasing)	Reduction in obesity or smoking

be achieved by a large project, but generation of economic activity along the route will be needed to justify the investment (business transformation) and there should be preparation to change societal behaviours to take advantage of this new capability for travel.

Similarly, a private sector organization that invests heavily in a new logistics infrastructure will expect benefits to be managed, which could involve process changes, organizational structure changes and cultural acceptance of a different approach.

As such, the programme manager has to deliver the means to change thus allowing transformation to take place, whereas the BCM is likely to be far more heavily involved with delivering the business transformation and political/societal aspects of a programme, as these are where the benefits will be generated. The programme manager and BCM roles are about working in partnership, delivering change and releasing benefits. They are mutually dependent on each other: neither can realize the benefits on their own. For the programme manager, developing good relationships with the BCMs is critical.

Figure 1.2 is critical to understanding the difference between the programme manager and BCM roles. The boxes on the left show what the programme manager delivers while the boxes on the right show what the BCM delivers. As you can see, the roles are fundamentally different in their focus.

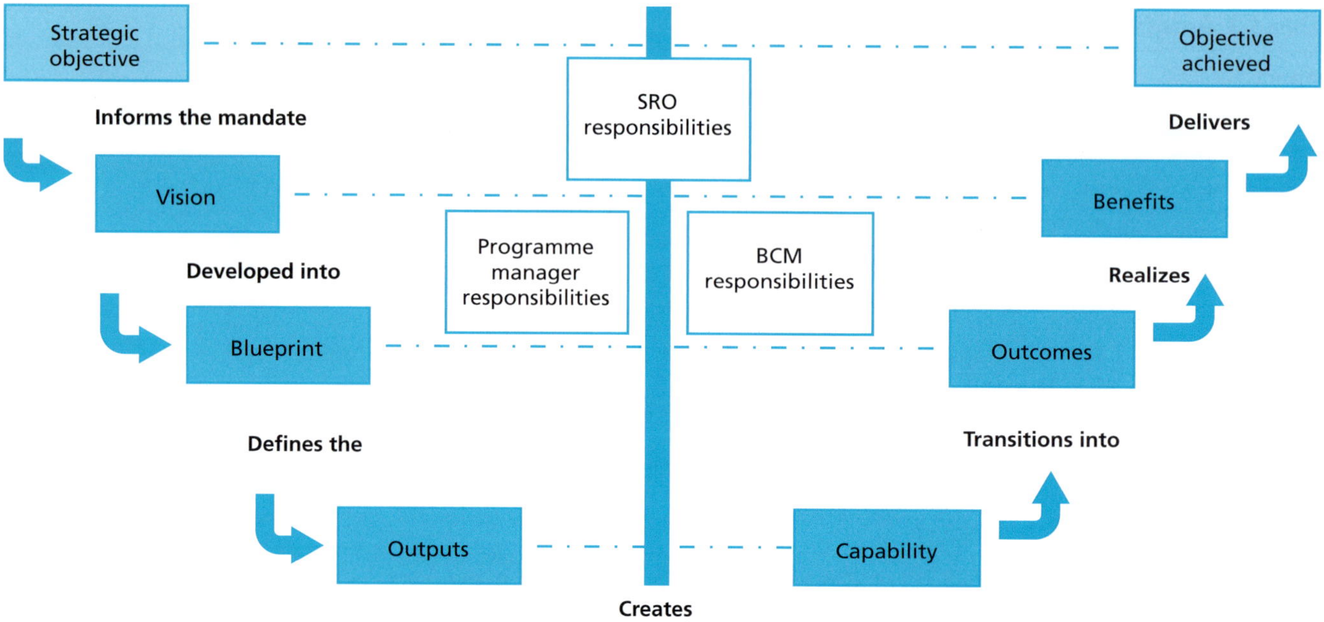

Figure 1.2 Programme delivery responsibilities

Programmes normally serve to deliver corporate objectives, as shown in the list below:

- The corporate objectives drive the development of the programme vision.
- The vision is expanded into a blueprint for the future organization.
- The blueprint defines what the projects need to create.
- The projects deliver outputs, which create capabilities.
- The capabilities are transitioned into outcomes.
- The outcomes enable the realization of benefits.
- The benefits are then achieved and contribute to the achievement of the corporate objectives.

1.4 HAVE YOU ACTUALLY GOT A PROGRAMME?

There is often a bit of a problem with the 'P' word. This is because organizations fail to actually define what it means to them. There are three main concepts that lurk around the P word:

- Portfolio
- Programmes
- Projects.

They are distinct and quite different from one another, but there are also a number of similarities.

The standard definitions from the AXELOS common glossary are:

- A **portfolio** is 'the totality of an organization's investment (or segment thereof) in the changes required to achieve its strategic objectives' and **portfolio management** is 'a coordinated collection of strategic processes and decisions that together enable the most effective balance of organizational change and business as usual'. If your programme has no end date or looks to be continual, you may well have a portfolio.
- A **programme** is defined as 'a temporary, flexible organization created to coordinate, direct and oversee the implementation of a set of related projects and activities in order to deliver outcomes and benefits related to the organization's strategic objectives. A programme is likely to have a life that spans several years.' Programmes deal with outcomes; projects deal with outputs.
- A **project** is 'a temporary organization that is created for the purpose of delivering one or more business products according to an agreed business case'. A particular project may or may not be part of a programme.

Programme management and project management are complementary approaches rather than alternatives, which is sometimes the interpretation. During a programme lifecycle, projects are initiated, run and closed. Programmes provide an umbrella under which these projects can be coordinated.

Hints and tips

There are many examples of project failures that can be seen as programme successes: for example Eurotunnel and Wembley Stadium. Both failed the classic project tests of delivering on time, within cost and to the required quality but are national successes.

There is also a really useful framework called the Portfolio, Programme and Project Management Maturity Model (P3M3®), which is a model for assessing the maturity of the organization (see section 10.2.1.2). P3M3 uses a number of perspectives that are common to all three disciplines, namely:

- Organizational governance
- Management control
- Benefits management
- Risk management
- Stakeholder management
- Finance management
- Resource management.

As can be seen, there are a lot of areas that are common, and it is easy to make the wrong choice without appropriate experience.

A maturity assessment using P3M3 would be very valuable for you. It will provide an analysis of your organization's maturity; the lower the maturity the lower the formality and support that will be available to you as a programme manager, which increases your personal risk exposure.

1.5 WHAT DOES ALL THIS MEAN TO YOU?

Well, it means you need to be careful about what you are being asked to contribute to and how effective you can be in the performance of your role.

It is quite common for the word 'programme' to be used to describe things that aren't programmes, so you might like to look through the following checklist of things that can cause confusion:

- It not just a big project; programmes have to deal with uncertainty and find the optimum solutions to deliver change and realize the desired benefits. As programme manager you will be the pathfinder.
- Has it got a start and end or is it continual? If it is continual, it is more likely to be a portfolio.
- Is the term 'programme of work' used? If so, it is more likely to be an ongoing investment in refurbishment or maintenance.
- Is it scoped to deliver transformational change? If not, then it is more likely to be a project, and the BCM is actually the customer for the products.
- Is it being driven by the need to change or the need to build something? If it is the latter then it will be more likely to operate like a project.

1.6 WHAT IS MSP?

As much of the guidance here is based on the MSP framework, it is helpful to understand the basic ideas. MSP is made up of principles, themes and a lifecycle called the transformational flow (Figure 1.3).

1.6.1 The principles

These are self-validating, universal and empowering, and apply to all aspects of delivery:

- **Remaining aligned with corporate strategy** A programme is typically a large investment that should make a significant contribution towards achieving corporate performance targets. A well-managed programme maintains good links with a sometimes volatile corporate strategy.
- **Leading change** Seeing through change in a programme is a leadership challenge. In addition to the need to manage a large number of complex tasks, people need to be led. It is impossible to move to a better future without clear leadership.
- **Envisioning and communicating a better future** A programme is relevant where there is a need to achieve transformational change, where there is some marked step change or break with the present required in the future capability. In order to achieve such a beneficial future state, the leaders of a programme must first describe a clear vision of that future.
- **Focusing on the benefits and threats to them** Best-practice programme management aligns everything towards satisfying strategic objectives by realizing the end benefits. Thus the programme's boundary, including the projects and activities that become part of the programme, are determined to enable the realization of these end benefits. The ultimate success of a programme is judged by its ability to realize these benefits and their continuing relevance to the strategic context. If the benefits are of strategic value, then effective risk management is crucial.
- **Adding value** A programme only remains valid if it adds value to the sum of its constituent projects and major activities. If it is found to add nothing then it is better to close the programme and allow the projects to proceed independently, coordinated by corporate portfolio management.
- **Designing and delivering a coherent capability** The programme will deliver a business architecture or final capability. This should have such internal coherence that all quality requirements are optimized, being released into operational use according to a schedule delivering maximum incremental capability with minimal adverse operational impact.

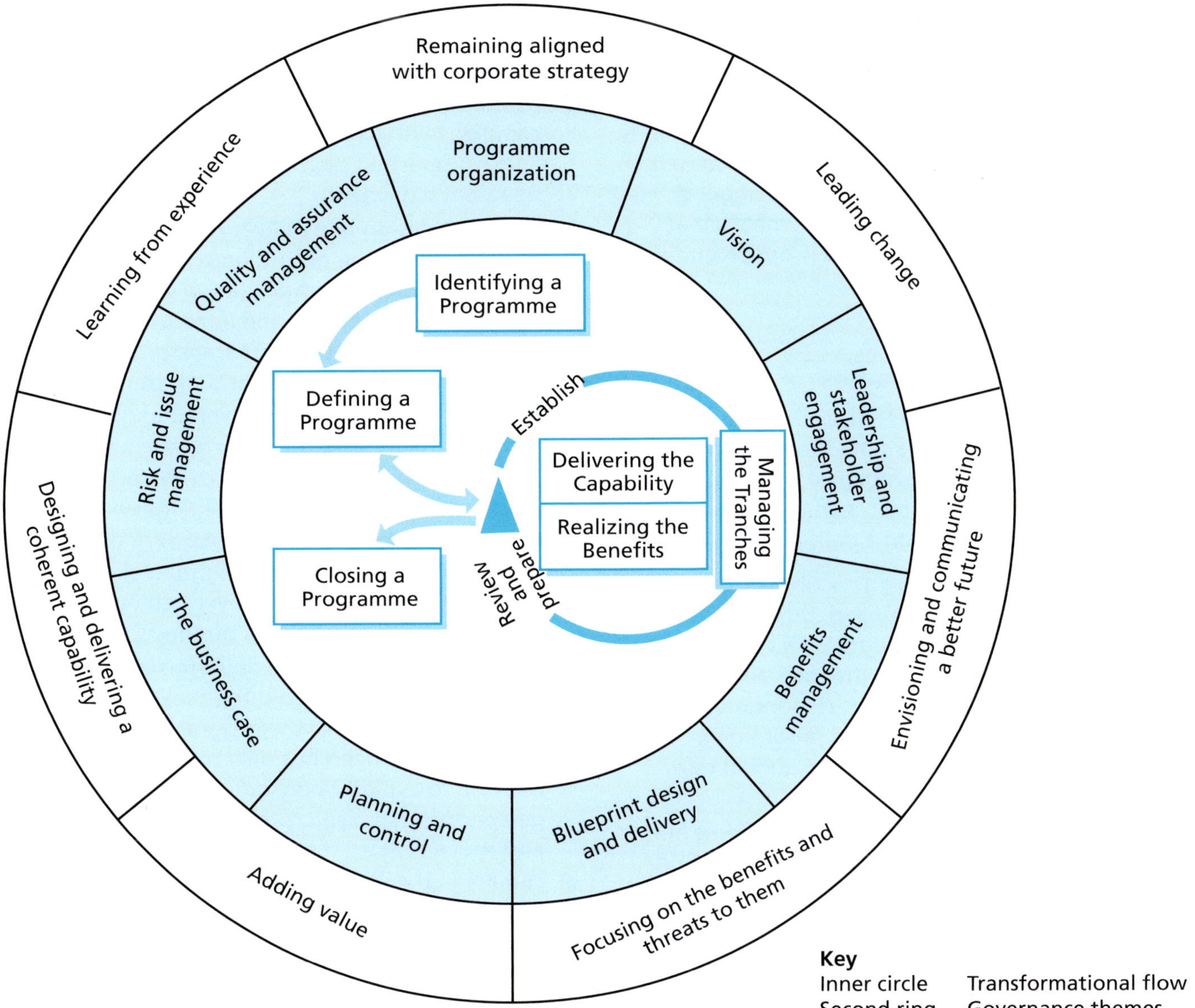

Figure 1.3 MSP framework and concepts

- **Learning from experience** A programme is a learning organization in that it reflects upon and improves its own performance during its life. Good governance requires approaches to managing the different themes that are regularly adjusted and adapted on the basis of experience and results so far. For example, part of good benefits realization management means that stakeholders are identifying new opportunities to realize benefits as their awareness and experience increases.

1.6.2 Governance themes

The themes are a set of references that explain how key elements of the programme should be delivered during its lifecycle. The governance themes cover subjects that will need to be constantly managed to a greater or lesser extent on a daily basis:

- **Programme organization** Describes how governance should be applied, through the sponsoring group and programme board, and provides guidance on the roles and responsibilities for the senior responsible owner, business change manager and programme manager. It also recommends additional roles.
- **Vision** Is required for the delivery of any programme; MSP sets out the key contents and how it should paint a picture of a better future for the organization.
- **Leadership and stakeholder engagement** Is critical to any programme because change requires effective leadership. MSP emphasizes the need to identify and communicate with stakeholders and provides analysis tools to generate greater understanding of their needs, perceptions and priorities.
- **Benefits management** Is the core difference between projects and programmes. The active exploitation of the opportunities that are offered by the investment in projects' deliverables is complex, with each benefit having its own profile and a supporting plan to deliver the changes and release the dividend.
- **Blueprint design and delivery** Form the foundation for the programme; what is the 'to-be' state for the organization when the programme completes, and in fact what is our starting point ('as-is' state)? Transformation is delivered in step changes through tranches.
- **Planning and control** Are covered in detail to explain how to develop the programme plan and maintain internal control of the projects to ensure that the programme remains on course.
- **The business case** Will be in place for all programmes, with MSP highlighting the need for the programme to have an overarching case, and each project having its own business case too.
- **Risk and issue management** Offers advice and guidance on how to avoid the realization of events that will cause the programme to fail. It focuses on the need not only to manage threats, but also to exploit opportunities. There are four perspectives: strategic, programme, operation and project risk.
- **Quality and assurance management** Describes how there should be optimal management of people, resources, suppliers, processes, assets, information and strategic alignment, and the importance of having an effective assurance strategy, to help enable and optimize the achievement of the programme goals.

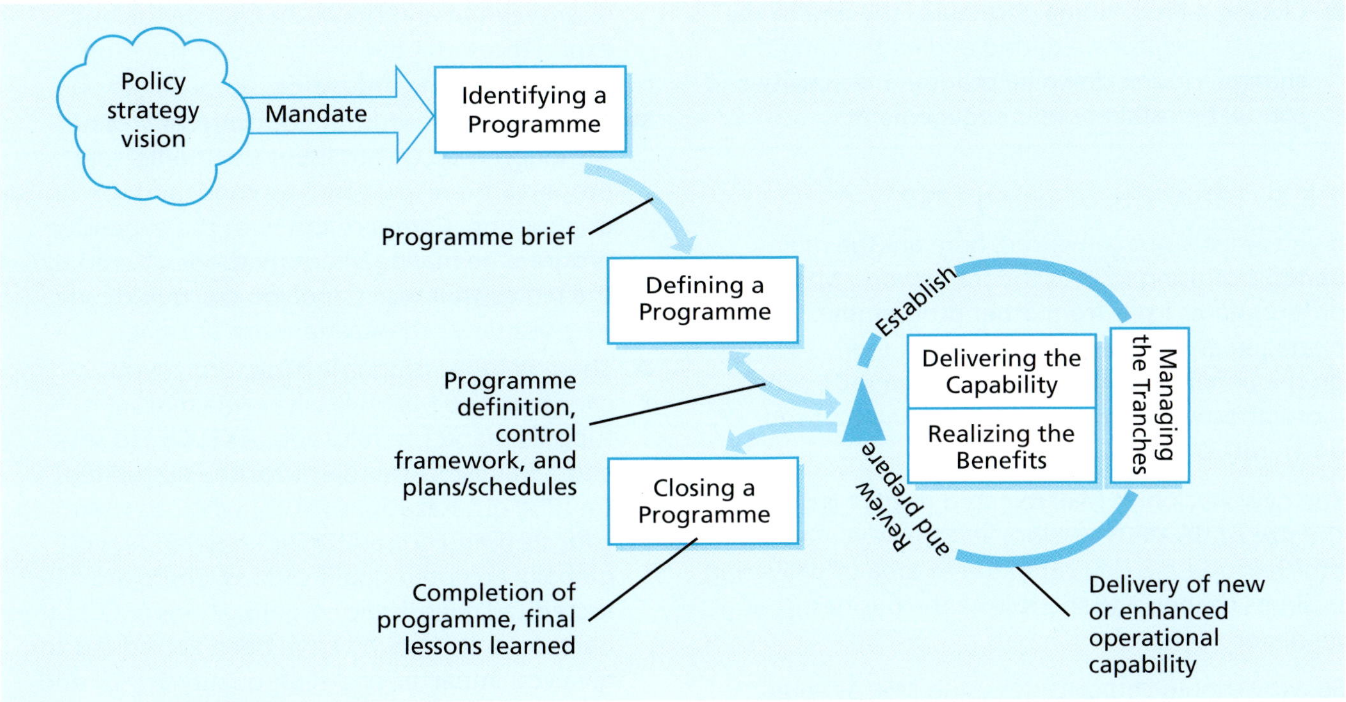

Figure 1.4 MSP transformational flow

1.6.3 Transformational flow

Transformational flow is the term used to describe the lifecycle of the programme; it uses 'flow' to reflect the evolving nature of the journey the programme takes and the adjustments that will need to be made. The following list summarizes the stages it passes through (see Figure 1.4):

- **Identifying a Programme** Takes an outline idea and undertakes analysis of stakeholders, clarification of the strategic requirements and market consultation to turn it into a business concept that gains strategic support.
- **Defining a Programme** Confirms the vision, undertakes detailed analysis of options and designs the programme infrastructure to deliver, resulting in a business case and strategic commitment.
- **Managing the Tranches** Describes the cyclical activities involved in managing and proving the coordinating interface between projects, business change and strategic direction.
- **Delivering the Capability** Explains how the alignment of the projects and other activities that deliver the blueprint will be managed and controlled.
- **Realizing the Benefits** Outlines the preparing, delivering and reviewing activities that will take the capability delivered by projects, transition it into the business operations and embed it within the business operations to release the intended benefits.

- **Closing a Programme** Structures the end to the programme, consolidating and embedding the change, closing down all programme activity and completing stakeholder engagement.

1.6.4 Benefits of using MSP

If you are still not convinced, here are the main benefits of using MSP as the framework. MSP differentiates itself from other programme management frameworks because it really focuses on the benefits from strategic change rather than more effective project delivery, coming at it top-down rather than bottom-up.

The new version of MSP released in 2011 is double the size of the 2003 version, and the vast majority of this increase is dedicated to the area of delivering business change and the role of the business change manager.

So, why should you consider using MSP as your programme management framework?

- **It is flexible and adaptable** MSP is not a methodology that you implement: it needs to be adapted and applied carefully and thoughtfully. It may be that not all the elements of MSP will be needed in your organization and it can be blended to fit with other frameworks. If you are using PMI, APM (Association for Project Management) or PRINCE2® (PRojects IN Controlled Environments) for your project management delivery, each will happily work with MSP.
- **It is proven and established** MSP has been around for more than 12 years now; it has been proven globally in the public and private sectors. Many of the problems identified from failed programmes would have been avoided if MSP had been applied. MSP is in a cycle of continual improvement and draws on knowledge and experiences as it evolves in one of the most rapidly changing industries.
- **It is free to use without licensing constraints** Although AXELOS Ltd owns the intellectual property, there are very few constraints on its use or adoption. Compare this with the expensive programme management methods offered by the big consultancies and you can quickly see why so many organizations are using it.
- **There is supporting infrastructure** If you choose to use MSP there is now a mature support market to help you. AXELOS Ltd sets and administers standards for the accredited training organizations (ATOs) who can train your staff and accredit their knowledge with globally accepted qualifications. There are accredited consultancy organizations (ACOs) that have consultants who have been accredited to give you impartial and high-quality advice and support to enable implementation. The best ones will be able to offer toolkits to help with implementation and get your organization up and running quickly and effectively.
- **It is part of the portfolio of best-practice guidance** The UK government has a long-term commitment to the best-practice product set which provides you with sustainability. These products are becoming more and more consistent and are part of a cycle of improvements that will bring them more closely together.

There is an old saying 'No one ever got sacked for choosing IBM', and the same probably applies to the best-practice products. There is a well-established global industry that is enabling organizations using it to go from strength to strength. Hopefully, the five reasons listed above will provide you with the justification to set your strategic direction.

PART 1
The governance themes

2 Introduction to the governance themes

2 Introduction to the governance themes

'The quality of everything we do depends on the quality of the thinking we do first. The quality of our thinking depends on the way we treat each other while we are thinking.'
Nancy Kline

The MSP governance themes are a set of references that explain how key elements of the programme should be delivered during its delivery lifecycle. They cover subjects that will need to be constantly managed, to a greater or lesser extent, on a daily basis during the lifecycle of the programme.

The nine MSP governance themes are dealt with in Chapters 3 to 10, but note that the order in which they are covered in this publication relates to the priorities of the programme manager rather than the order of the MSP guide. Visions and blueprints are combined in one chapter (Chapter 4).

Example

Many people in management are in too much of a rush. Go slowly now to speed up later is a culture being actively promoted by Nancy Kline in *Time to Think*. This is one approach that is producing good results, which are just as applicable to programmes as any other form of management.

Some feedback reported by clients after adopting the 'thinking environment' in their culture:

- We saved 62% of senior management meeting time.
- We reduced by 44% the cost of each decision.
- We prevented, in 30 minutes, a month of research work.
- We rescued a £90,000,000 product in less than an hour.
- Because of our use of the thinking environment, the quality of life for this team now is exceptional. How can you put a monetary value on having people openly demonstrate respect towards one another?
- We now have inspiring, energetic, focused meetings with impressive outcomes. This is because everyone is thinking and contributing.

Source: www.timetothink.com/thinking-environment/

The themes generally have a cycle of activities (see Figure 2.1). These are consistent and help us to understand some of the documentation, for

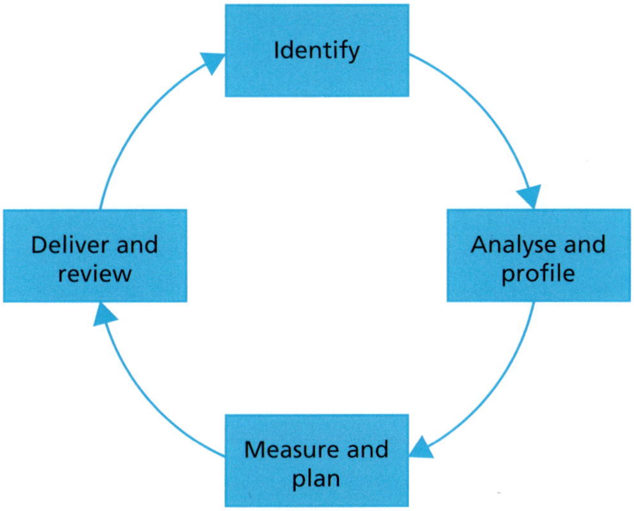

Figure 2.1 Typical theme lifecycle

example risk management. Risks will be identified and analysed, with the information recorded in the risk register. The plan to mitigate and manage the risks is then developed, the activities are undertaken and their effectiveness reviewed.

These strategies are absolutely critical to your role; without them you have no control. The strategies have rather grand names; basically you are creating some rules and a framework that will enable the programme to operate.

> *'If at first you don't succeed, try management.'*
> Geof Leigh

The strategies set out how you will manage the eight core themes that will lead to programme success. Even though MSP says that they are assembled during Defining the Programme, you will need some of them much sooner than that.

The strategies set out how the programme will manage a number of key areas. In organizations which run programmes regularly, lots of information will exist so all you will need to do is conform, or work out where there are gaps or where your programme may struggle to comply for some reason.

The strategies evolve over the life of the programme; they will be relatively light touch in the beginning when the direction is more abstract, but as the programme moves into tranche delivery mode controls will tighten up considerably.

There are nine strategies (see Table 2.1), and they tend to cover a lot of common areas. MSP does not intend that you sit down and laboriously write out each heading; it is quite common to have all the strategies in one document to avoid repetition.

Hints and tips

Poor strategies and plans will mean that things are done in the wrong way and at the wrong time – not a recipe for success.

One of the key roles of the strategies, which is often misunderstood, is that they define how the programme will interact with projects. They define the project-related interfaces, standards and controls that will be in place; so for example, the issue management strategy will define how projects will manage their issues, the triggers and escalation routes they will use to manage them.

Most of the strategies have an associated plan – the idea being that you don't write the strategy and forget to implement it. It can be built into the strategy document as the implementation plan or built into the programme plan activities. The important thing is that the strategy has to be implemented, managed and reviewed for effectiveness at appropriate moments.

In this introductory chapter on the governance themes, we are discussing the common areas that the strategies cover. In the individual chapters we cover anything specific that you should be considering. The common areas are:

- **Roles and responsibilities** In most cases these are consistent; the SRO is accountable, you do a lot of the design and management while the business change managers (BCMs) provide the gateway to operational and stakeholder groups. There are exceptions to this: noticeably around benefits and stakeholders, where the BCMs are more dominant.

Table 2.1 The programme manager's engagement with strategy documents

Stakeholders' engagement strategy	This defines how the stakeholders will be engaged; it is critical to you as you are responsible for the oversight of all engagement and communications for the programme. Many other roles will do the communicating but it is you who must make sure it is effective.
Resources management strategy	This outlines where the resources for the programme are coming from. You are going to need the support of other managers to work out if they are going to be external or internal and how they are going to be acquired and/or released from the business.
Risk management strategy	You will need to ensure that all risks are fully covered by the strategy. There is a danger that some risks such as operational will sit in a parallel environment and may be overlooked by the programme as it focuses on project-related matters: make sure this doesn't happen.
Issues management strategy	Make sure you don't just focus on programme and project delivery matters. Issues to do with changing the organization, including staff resistance, will also be important.
Quality and assurance strategy	This may well be in line with your organization's assurance approach. Make sure you look beyond the delivery of project outputs. The programme will only succeed if the outputs are used properly. An area that you should also keep an eye out for is assurance that your organization is actually prepared for the change. You need to have some mechanism in place for testing its readiness.
Monitoring and control strategy	This one tends to be focused on the internal processes of the programme and how it controls its projects. Your main concern is that the project will deliver the outputs on time and to the right standard, so you should treat operational areas like a customer for this one.
Organization structure	The structure of the programme will evolve through the various tranches and this document outlines how the structure will cope, as opposed to the resource management strategy which outlines where the resources will come from. Make sure it is clear what skills and experience are needed.
Benefits management strategy	Although this is written by you, this document is the bread and butter for the BCM. It is your responsibility to develop it only because governance is your responsibility. The actual content is the BCM's. You must collaborate extensively with BCMs on this.
Information management strategy	This one is concerned with the effectiveness of information management and the maintenance of its accuracy. Consider this carefully; without good data and information you and the rest of the team are managing blind.

- **Tools and templates** In many organizations these will exist, but things such as highlight reports, risk registers and planning templates will exist or there may be tracking tools in place that you require people to follow. However, if not you will have to create them: so for each strategy you will define what will be used, when and by whom.
- **Processes** These will be illustrated in the strategy so that people know how they are expected to operate; they will include the internal programme processes and also how the projects and operations will interface with the programme.
- **Corporate standards** These could be industry-related, e.g. ISO 14001 or specific to the organization, such as procurement.
- **Internal standards** Standards that apply to the programme can range from the financial measures you will use for benefits, or how levels of risk exposure will be reported. These have to be consistent across the programme and its projects.
- **Terms and vocabulary** This can be troublesome if people have different interpretations, so they should be defined.
- **Interfaces with other groups** This is where the obligations and agreements with other groups are made available: for example terms of references with suppliers, operating agreements with other programmes or a portfolio office on tasks.
- **Success measures** What you would like the programme to be judged on in this context: so for example, what would effective and efficient risk management be measured against?
- **Escalation procedures** What will trigger an escalation? What will the escalation route be if, for example, there is a change to a benefit value? It should also define what would trigger the escalation, e.g. 10% deviation.

The stakeholder management theme is a good example of how the documentation tends to work (Figure 2.2). The stakeholder management strategy sets out the framework within which the programme will operate and deliver stakeholder management. The stakeholder profiles are detailed descriptions about each stakeholder (including their interests and influences) and how the programme will engage with them. The communications plan is the tracking device to ensure your stakeholder engagement is managed effectively.

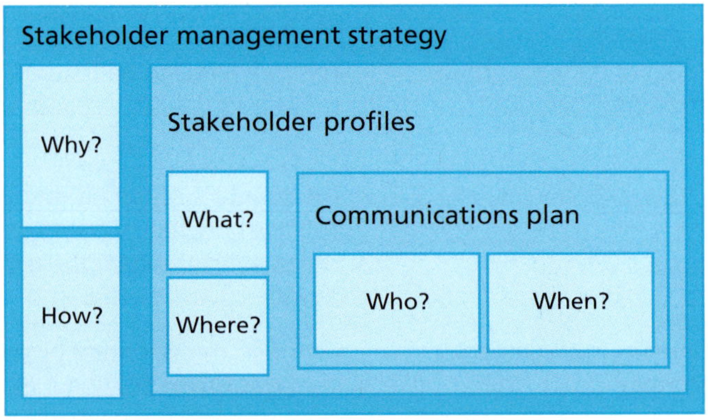

Figure 2.2 Stakeholder management theme documentation

3 Programme organization

3 Programme organization

This chapter summarizes the MSP guidance on programme organization structures. It interprets the structure to help you work out how your responsibilities as the programme manager are critical and require careful interpretation. Is it also important to remember that the programme manager can only achieve success by working successfully with other roles. In the programme the most notable role that the programme manager will need to work with is likely to be the business change manager (BCM). The BCM represents those parts of the organization that the programme will change. If an improved future organization is not forthcoming the programme will almost certainly fail.

The designing of your team will in many ways be the defining moment for the programme. There are many things you need to consider. A common error is to assume that project managers will make good programme managers: this is simply not the case and it is more about behaviours. Cranfield produced a paper in 2005 (Attributes and Levels of Programme Management Competence: An Interpretive Study) which provided valuable insights into programme management perceptions. It explained that there were four types of programme manager, and they range through four levels:

- **Level 1** Concern for delivery of programme scope and focused on detail of project delivery
- **Level 2** Concern for wider organizational impact of programme but primarily focused on the delivery of the project
- **Level 3** Concern for achievement of high-level programme outcomes and focused on the achievement of benefits
- **Level 4** Concern for development of strategic capabilities and the wider context of the programme.

We have found this a really useful insight into understanding the different types of programme managers and when they are needed during the programme lifecycle. If you are a level 1 at the start of a programme you will quickly get into project delivery and probably lose the strategic context. If you are a level 4 during the delivery phase of a complex programme, it is likely the controls are weak and you will be bored. Consequently it highlights the need to plan for different programme managers at different stages of the programme.

The programme manager oversees all the projects, so good relationships with key project roles are also critical. The design of the programme organization should be done as a whole to make sure the roles are complementary, not contradictory, and that the relationships between roles are clear.

3.1 BASIC PRINCIPLES

The programme governance model is relatively straightforward; it is a three-layer model of control (see Figure 3.1).

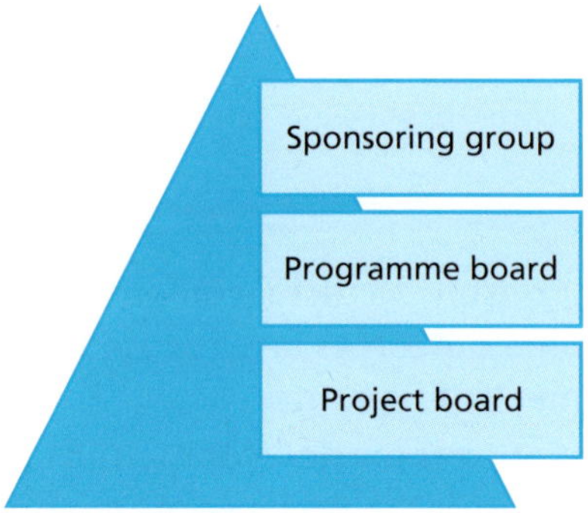

Figure 3.1 Programme governance layers

There is a sponsoring group that sits at the top of the structure and sets the strategic direction for the programme.

The second tier is the group that is responsible for delivering the strategy or objective. This is called the programme board and it is where you sit in the organization. The programme board is responsible for delivering the new capability (normally through projects) and, equally important, the anticipated benefits from the investment.

The third tier is the project, which normally has a control group, maybe referred to as the project board. There will be a number of these and this is where direct control of the projects is applied; this takes the strain off the programme board, which should be the escalation point when the projects have problems.

The relationship between core roles in MSP and these three layers of control is shown in Figure 3.2.

The senior responsible owner (SRO) is the interface to the sponsoring level, which could be the corporate or portfolio board; the names will vary between organizations. The SRO is accountable for achieving the parts of business strategy relevant to the programme.

Hints and tips

The programme board is not just a stakeholder group, it is a decision-making body: so everyone attending should have the authority to influence or make a decision.

At the programme level, there is the programme manager, namely you, who should have direct control of the project resources. Your role is

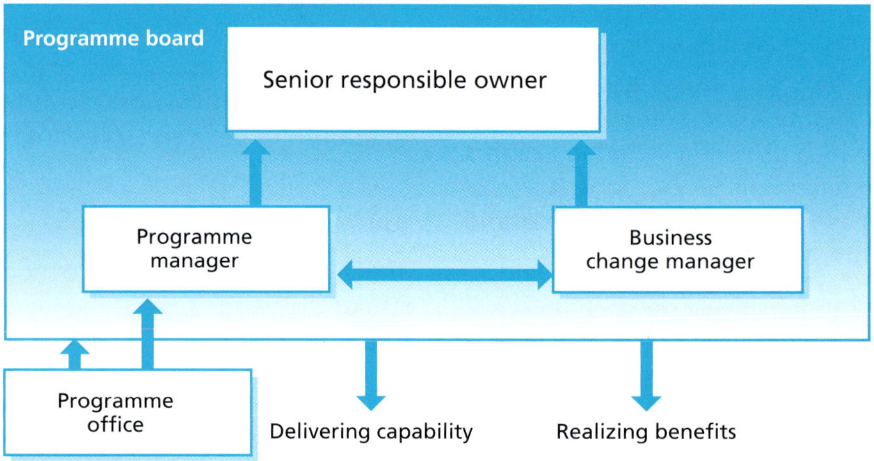

Figure 3.2 Programme roles

principally to deliver the capability and manage the governance and controls of the programme.

The composition of the programme team will vary depending on where you are in the programme lifecycle and which activity is being undertaken. You will play a key part in determining what the composition of the team should be as the next set of activities approaches. You may require help to find the people who have the right skills and experience. Consider approaching the BCM for people with operation skills, and specialist managers such as IT, facilities, legal etc. You should also involve HR.

The BCM represents the areas to be changed, designing how the organization will work in the future and delivering the benefits from the change. In simple terms, BCM is the customer for whatever the programme will create, so you are critical in defining what they will require.

Hints and tips

Watch out for programme boards that are dominated by discussions around projects. If that is the case, they are trying to do the project board's job rather than their own.

> *'Change will not come if we wait for some other person, or if we wait for some other time. We are the ones we've been waiting for. We are the change that we seek.'* Barack Obama

3.2 WHAT DOES MSP HAVE TO SAY?

Just for the record, we note below how MSP describes each of these roles. There is a long list of responsibilities for each of them in Chapter 4 of the full guide, but this summary captures the spirit of what it has to say.

3.2.1 Sponsoring group

The sponsoring group represents those senior managers who are responsible for:

- The investment decision
- Defining the direction of the business
- Ensuring the ongoing overall alignment of the programme with the strategic direction of the organization.

The sponsoring group will appoint the SRO who, as part of the sponsoring group, is likely to be a peer of the other members. The role of the sponsoring group may well be performed by an existing executive committee or other board of the organization.

3.2.2 Senior responsible owner

The SRO is accountable for the programme, ensuring that it meets its objectives and realizes the expected benefits. The individual who fulfils this role should be able to lead the programme board with energy and drive, and must be empowered to direct the programme and take decisions. They must have enough seniority and authority to provide leadership to the programme team and take on accountability for delivery.

3.2.3 Programme board

Established by the SRO, often early in the programme (e.g.in the Identify step), the prime purpose of the programme board will be to drive the programme forward and deliver the outcomes and benefits. Members will provide resources and specific commitment to support the SRO, who is accountable for the successful delivery of the programme.

The programme board reports to the SRO. While the SRO may delegate responsibilities and action to members of the programme board, its existence does not dilute the SRO's accountabilities and decision-making authority.

Programme board members must take the lead in supporting the authority and control of the SRO over the programme as a whole, including ensuring appropriate coordination across the projects and activities that comprise the programme. You and the BCMs should be members of the programme board.

3.2.4 Programme manager

The programme manager is responsible for leading and managing the programme from establishing the programme through to delivery of the new capabilities, realization of benefits and programme closure. The programme manager has primary responsibility for successful delivery of the new capabilities and establishing governance. The BCM is responsible for benefits realization via the organizational adoption and usage of the capability and transition to the desired outcome.

The programme manager will normally be appointed as part of forming the team for Defining a Programme, though it is important that someone assumes the role of programme manager when the programme brief and plans for programme definition (programme preparation plan) are being developed in Identifying a Programme.

3.2.5 Business change manager

The role of the BCM is primarily benefits-focused. The BCM is responsible, on behalf of the business operations and the SRO, for:

- Defining the benefits
- Defining the future operating state of the business area they represent
- Assessing progress towards Realizing the Benefits
- Achieving measured improvements
- Monitoring performance.

This need to define and realize benefits in terms of measured improvements in business performance means that the BCM must be 'business-side' in order to provide a bridge between the programme and business operations.

The programme manager is responsible for Delivering the Capability, while the BCM is responsible for Realizing the [resultant] Benefits by embedding that capability into business operations and facilitating business changes to exploit that capability. The individuals appointed to each role must be able to work in close partnership to ensure that the right capabilities are delivered and that they are put to best use.

If a programme is implementing change across different parts of an organization, each should nominate a BCM. An integral part of the BCM role is an intimate knowledge of, and credibility in, the operational business.

3.2.6 Business change team

A business change team can be formed to help each of the BCMs take their stakeholders in their operational areas through the change cycle. Such a team considers the interests of those parts of the organization to be changed and will ensure that they are thoroughly prepared for the transition. The team's focus is on helping the operational unit through transition as smoothly as possible. It is a support function for when operational people need the most help.

A business change team can be useful to you as programme manager. If there are lots of BCMs you may need to develop and maintain close relationships with all of them – sometimes a daunting task. If there is a business change team it will have a leader (business change authority). Your primary relationship is with the leader and should be more straightforward to manage.

3.2.7 Programme office

Programmes are major undertakings, often affecting large numbers of people and organizations and generating a substantial volume of information. The nerve centre and information hub is the programme office. All information, communication, monitoring and control activities for the programme are coordinated through the programme office.

Treat the programme office as your best friend. They can be invaluable, taking away much of the administration and leaving you time to think and deal with people. But they are much more than this. They can be your extended eyes and ears, not just on your programme but bringing in a wealth of intelligence about how other change initiatives have fared. They can help you deploy good practice and develop competencies. And like any best friend you should encourage them to be honest with you and tell you when you are not performing well.

3.2.8 Programme assurance

Assurance is the assessment to generate confidence that the programme is being managed effectively and that it is on track to realize the expected benefits and achieve the desired outcomes. Assurance, like audit, should be carried out independently of the programme management team.

3.3 WHAT DOES THIS MEAN TO YOU?

Hopefully this has given a flavour for where your role sits in the programme's structure and that it is pivotal in achieving programme success. During programme start-up, often the temptation is to concentrate on launching projects. The business change aspect is put on the back burner as it is months or years away. The flaw in this logic is that business change isn't thought about until it is too late, at which point failure looms. There is a lot of critical work to do outside of projects to make the organization fully prepared for transition. You need to work closely with the BCMs on this.

3.3.1 Organizational design

The BCM(s) and programme manager are normally peers who report to the SRO. But the programme manager has many and often complex relationships. Figure 3.3 and the following list show some examples of these relationships:

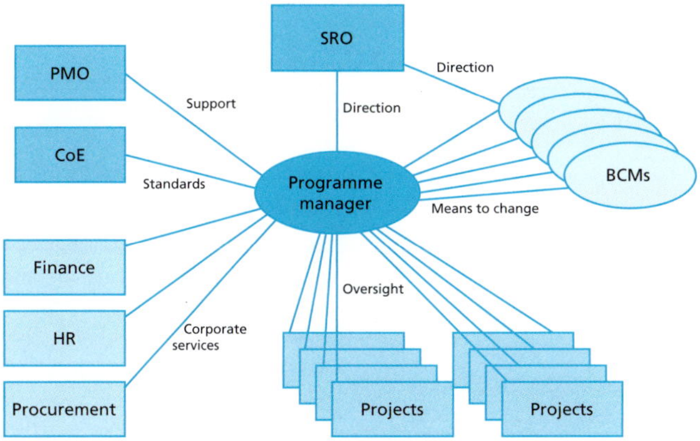

Figure 3.3 Examples of programme manager relationships

- The programme manager and the BCM will report to the SRO.
- The programme manager works in partnership with the BCMs to design the future organization, develop the means to change it and implement the changes to realize benefits.
- Projects should not be micro-managed but the programme manager will start them, oversee their progress and close them, maintaining overall control.
- A programme management office (PMO) can provide support for the programme and may report to the programme manager.
- A centre of excellence (CoE) is likely to be independent and can apply scrutiny via audit or assurance.
- Links to corporate functions are needed to provide services to the programme and to tie programme and corporate governance together.

The skills that you will need in your programme will depend on the programme, but it is easy to miss the obvious so consider things such as:

- Procurement
- Supply chain negotiation
- Specialist knowledge, construction, IT, health and safety etc.
- Legal
- Communication
- Operational support such as help desks, facilities management.

It is really important that you do not try to become a jack of all trades: being a good-quality programme manager requires focus.

3.3.2 Decision-making authority

MSP uses the RACI model (Responsible, Accountable, Consulted, Informed), which works very well in the guide but you need to think more precisely and so

Table 3.1 The 5As Model (©Aspire Europe)

Authorize	Has the ultimate authority to make the final decision; this would normally be the SRO within the programme context.
Approve	Clearly part of the decision-making process, so will endorse the decision and back it, or chose not to back it, leaving the authorizer to override if needed. Will often be associated with the BCM, as they are making the calls on behalf of the business.
Action	Responsible for getting a job done or preparatory work that will need approval. This will often be with the programme manager or your team, in particular project managers.
Advise	This is someone who will provide specific expertise or help. Your programme office will do this a lot: for example as part of the risk management process. So this would cover people with no authority but who have knowledge to contribute.
Assure	This is independent assessment, so their comments have authority but you may choose not to heed them. However, this would be unwise unless you have a good reason. Using the risk example, it could be the corporate risk team who review your risk management.

will the SRO: so we have produced a model (see Table 3.1). When there are multiple people with 'responsibility', decision-making can get blurred. A particular problem area is consultation: are you asking someone for approval, endorsement or just acknowledgement that you are doing something? Most of all, what happens if they disagree?

The model that we have produced at Aspire Europe is more focused than RACI and easier to translate. We call it the '5As Model' and have used it to help a number of organizations, particularly where there are multiple layers in a portfolio, and programmes and projects can get very confused.

3.3.3 Terms of reference

For each role you will need to ensure that the person knows what is expected of them. It is very common to find these explanations missing or only very abstract descriptions, so make it real so that people know what is needed.

- Use the 5As Model to allocate responsibilities for the process area outputs, e.g. the risk register.
- Look for specific operational-related work that is specific to each BCM.
- Project teams should have their scope and authority clearly defined.

Areas that should be generically covered in each terms of reference include:

- Stop/go decisions on projects and other specific areas which need to be named
- Communications and stakeholder activities
- Managing the design of the future organization in a blueprint
- Delivery of the blueprint, via projects and other activities
- Planning and control
- Benefit analysis and integration with plans
- Risk and issue management
- Quality, assurance and audit
- Programme infrastructure
- Overseeing corporate performance metrics
- Business case achievement
- Programme office
- Information management
- Reporting
- The programme team, its structure, roles and appointments.

3.3.4 What about you?

Thinking of you personally, you must have terms of reference that are meaningful, relevant to the role and agreed with the SRO. The MSP guide has an extensive list of generic responsibilities but you need something more specific. Use the following checklist for your terms of reference:

- What resources are being put under your control – human, financial and physical?
- Is this programme your sole assignment? (If not, how will your time and priorities be divided?)
- Who do you report to and will the relationship work?

The next challenge is to understand what you have to do on your programme and what competencies you will need to have. Programmes are not all the same so don't assume the role will be exactly the same as you move from one assignment to the next.

The chief who has invited you to take this role of programme manager should be a member of the sponsoring group, and probably the corporate management team; he or she will also have discussed it with you directly, as you will have a reporting line to him or her.

Hints and tips

Get close to the BCM(s) and treat them as your best friend or partner: you can't achieve success without them.

It will be helpful if you have a sense of humour to go with your ambition, because the programme manager role is one of the toughest to find the right people for. The programme and project teams can be recruited from the external market. If you are a contract programme manager you will need to get close to the BCMs as soon as possible. They come from within the organization and they know how it ticks, the culture and the amount of change that can be driven through without causing performance to deteriorate – all critical knowledge if you are to be successful.

You will be expected to perform as an effective leader of change and to achieve this you will need to:

- Have the respect of the rest of the programme team and managers of those parts of the organization that will change.
- Establish effective working relationships, especially with the SRO and BCMs.
- Have personal belief in the strategy and objectives; if not, you could become a saboteur.
- Be able to sell the concepts to a wide range of stakeholders and set appropriate expectations.
- Have the self-belief to challenge direction if you do not believe the benefits and outcomes are achievable. Better to stop now than fail later.
- Be politically astute.
- Lead and direct many projects without micro-managing them but also keep them under control and focused on the benefits their outputs will enable.

You will also need to be able to:

- Control adequate resources
- Manage time and performance effectively to cope with the pressure for change
- Communicate effectively
- Negotiate effectively with your peers to achieve preferred solutions
- Build, manage and motivate a team
- Understand and manage the implications on operational performance
- Have sufficient time available: this is where support from a PMO can be invaluable.

3.3.4.1 Pitfalls to avoid

If you are asked to work on more than one initiative at a time, be wary of becoming overstretched. Here are some potential pitfalls to consider:

- One or more projects are struggling so you appoint yourself as project executive or, worse, as project manager. Not only does your workload increase, you are now trying to work in the detail of projects and keep a focus on the bigger picture of the programme. Consider coaching for the projects, or getting help from a PMO. If there are some expert project managers in the programme they might assist.
- Where there are many BCMs, it may not be sensible to try to develop working relationships with all of them. Is there a business change team? If so develop the relationship with the senior BCM (business change authority in MSP).
- Your role requires you to plan, coordinate, oversee and direct a substantial part of the programme. You will know a lot about managing projects. Don't try to become an expert at everything else. Engage and seek help from other experts: technical, operations,

legislative etc. If you do this right this should develop a sense of ownership in their part of the programme and they can become your champions. There may be times when you need all the allies you can get.

3.3.5 Building the capability

Once you have worked through your own role and understood the programme team structure then you will need to think about your contribution to building the capability of the team. The nature of the programme and previous experience will largely dictate what is required to build the capability. Here are some areas you should consider:

- **Skills and training** These will almost certainly be required and are often ignored. The team will need to have a good understanding of change management at the organization, team and individual levels. These are examples of skills needed:
  - Process mapping and documentation
  - Benefits management
  - Planning
  - Business performance management, e.g. Lean Six Sigma
  - Stakeholder and communications management
  - Project controls
  - Risk management
  - Technical knowledge of the change, the market or particular products or technology
  - Risk and issues
  - Configuration and information management
  - Governance
  - Data collection, analysis and reporting.
- **Team building and development** This is often overlooked when assembling temporary teams. A programme may well be in place for some years. It may need to establish values of its own. It will also be subject to regular change as different people are moved into and out from the team during the programme lifecycle, so the team must be adaptable to change itself.

3.4 YOUR ROLE IN SETTING UP THE PROGRAMME ORGANIZATION

This is what MSP describes as the 'areas of focus' in relation to the programme organization (see Table 3.2). In practice this means things you and the others listed below should do.

The relationships in a programme are complex; this is a quick summary of your relationship with the main roles and groups:

- **Sponsoring group** You will be a reporting line to one of the executives who are sponsoring the programme and you will be looking after their interests in the programme. You will probably have a direct report to someone on this group. As programme manager this is typically the SRO.
- **Senior responsible owner** Is accountable to the sponsoring group for the successful achievement of the programme objectives. Your job is to support him/her in that role and ensure that the change management controls are in place to keep them out of trouble.
- **BCMs** The potential for conflict between BCMs should not be underestimated. The needs of different parts of the organization or market are often in conflict and the BCMs will need to resolve these to their own satisfaction to ensure that it is clear what is required from the

Table 3.2 Areas of focus for the key roles in programme organization

Role	Area of focus
Senior responsible owner (SRO)	Ensuring that the programme has the necessary skills, resources and experience required to deliver the change Putting clear lines of authority in place Ensuring that sponsoring group members have a clear understanding of their roles Appointment of the programme manager Approval of the BCM appointment by the sponsoring group members
Programme manager	Design and appointment of the programme team Appointment of the programme office Facilitating the appointment of project management teams Ensuring that all roles have clearly defined responsibilities Ensuring that the organization design is managed through the programme lifecycle Induction of new members into the programme team Line management of the programme team Efficiency and competency of resources being deployed
Business change manager(s)	Design and appointment of the business change team Induction and management of members into the business change team Development and performance of the individuals in the business change team
Programme office	Advice and guidance on roles and responsibilities within the programme team Maintenance of organization information Support in recruitment and appointments

programme. Without this, programme boards will become places of significant conflict if there are competing demands that cannot be resolved.

- **Programme office** Principally supports you in the same way as the business change team supports the BCM. You will need to build a good relationship with them because they are the knowledge hub of the programme and will know where the issues are that may affect you. They will need information from you about stakeholders, risks, issues and business performance data; they will also be a good source of information for you on the progress of projects and potential issues that may be arising.
- **Programme assurance** Treat assurance roles as your friend; it is much better to keep them on the inside so they can help you. They will give you advice and guidance on the best approaches to handling problems and you can use them to undertake reviews of the readiness to change and make sure you are not being misled about how advanced preparations are.

- **Project teams and project boards** As programme manager you are likely to be heavily involved in setting up project governance. Projects are critical to the success of the programme. In programmes success is dependent on much more than project outputs passing technical testing. You will need to make sure that projects get enough operational input, organized via the BCM, so they understand the relationship between their outputs and benefits.

  You will need to set up a close working relationship with each project as your success is dependent on them, so a relationship based on trust is very important. The project executive is accountable to the programme board for the project and therefore likely to attend such meetings.

Now you should have a good idea of what is expected of you and the other roles; for many programmes, several aspects will need to be re-interpreted – not least the actual title, which may well vary.

Hints and tips

Avoid attending project boards, other than by exception: you will get sucked into their detail and undermine the governance.

4

Visions and blueprints

4 Visions and blueprints

> *'If we don't know where we are going, how will we know when we have arrived let alone how we are going to get there?'* Rod Sowden

Visions and blueprints are very important concepts as they set out the strategic direction for the programme and help to mobilize the change and provide the clarity about what the programme will actually deliver.

The vision has two aspects: there is the 'vision' that sets out the justification for the programme and what the world will be like at the end, and there is also the 'vision statement', which encapsulates the vision into a statement that provides the basis of communications. The vision may be expressed in different ways, so there may actually be different versions of the vision statement to meet the needs of different audiences. It is important that there is only one vision as there can only be one ending.

The blueprint is the definition of what the programme will deliver; it can also be referred to as the 'target operating model', but care needs to be taken with this term. There are many interpretations and there are many examples which definitely do not match up to the expectations of a programme blueprint.

The term 'outcomes' is used liberally in business speech. As a point of clarity, in programme management the outcomes are what happens when the blueprint comes to life. So, if the programme is talking about the outcomes it will deliver, then the blueprint should contain the detail behind these outcomes; if the blueprint doesn't exist at this stage, you may already be in trouble.

MSP deals with these concepts separately but in this publication they are covered together as they are inherently linked. There is also a link to benefits (see Figure 4.1) but benefits management is covered separately in Chapter 5. These three concepts are at the core of the programme manager role.

You will find further discussion of visions and blueprints in Chapter 5 of the *MSP Survival Guide for Business Change Managers*.

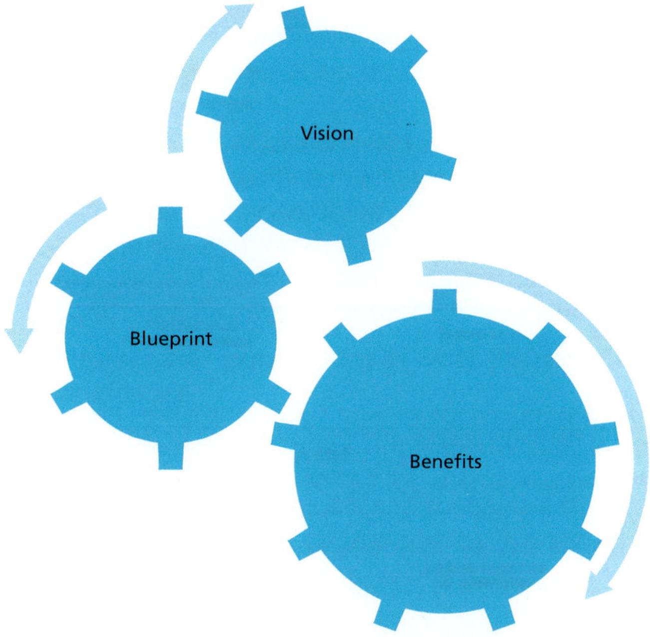

Figure 4.1 Vision, blueprint and benefits

4.1 BASIC PRINCIPLES

The **vision** (see section 4.2.1**)** is developed early in the programme and this is one of the main reasons that the business change manager (BCM) needs to be in place at the outset because if the vision is established without their involvement, then it may be difficult for you to get them to buy into it. If you don't make sure that key roles, especially BCMs, are committed to the vision you are not going to be very effective.

A good way to describe the role of the vision is that it acts as a 'beacon' for the programme, setting out the direction and justification for the change.

> **Example**
>
> At a local authority programme meeting, when members of a sponsoring group for a major cultural change programme were asked to explain the programme vision in their own words they struggled. They could all locate the vision and signpost others to it but giving it meaning and relating it to tangible outcomes was a challenge. They realized they had not been describing the organizational changes in a way that helped others understand the implications for them. They agreed to work together on compiling stories and examples to illustrate the similarities and differences between the current and the future culture.

The **blueprint** (see section 4.2.2**)** is the flip side of the vision; whereas the vision is setting out where the programme is going, the blueprint describes what it will be like when the programme arrives. It is where the detail of what will be left behind by the programme is stored.

The blueprint is your key document as it defines the difference between where you are today and the end state, which is the change you have to deliver. It details what services will be provided, how and who will provide them, what infrastructure needs to be in place and the information that will be used to manage it.

A common cause for programme failure is the lack of a blueprint, which means that the programme doesn't really know where it is going. The programme launches projects hopefully but there comes a point of revelation when someone realizes it doesn't all add up – quite often that someone is a BCM and by then too much money has been spent badly.

> **Hints and tips**
>
> The blueprint is critical; it contains the definition of what your organization's functions will look like after the change so it is essential that you own the detail. Without a blueprint it is not possible to effectively estimate benefits or what capability you will need.

Imagine you are on one of the TV property makeover shows. You have just bought a rundown building. You believe you can turn it into your dream home (your vision). You are not an architect or a builder, so you will need the help of these professionals. You will need to describe your dream home to the architect. What do you expect back: an artist's impressions or similar? When these are correct you have a vision statement. These can be used to help the builder and your family understand what the end result will look like.

The architect will need to develop designs for the builders. The starting point is understanding the current state of the building. This is the 'as-is' blueprint. The artist's impressions need to become a proper design for the building when it will be completed. This is the 'to-be' or final-state blueprint. But wait – you need to move into the property before it is complete to sell your existing house to raise funds to finish the job. So the architect is going to have to produce a design showing how some of the building can be completed first to give you adequate living space while the rest of the work is carried out. This is an intermediate blueprint. The two phases of construction are two tranches in MSP.

When you are comfortable with these designs and outline arrangements, the architect needs to develop them into more detail. This will be necessary for various reasons. Some will be legislative, for example to get planning permission from local authorities. Some will be used to instruct builders and suppliers on the detail.

So you now feel ready to start your house renovation – but wait. What about:

- **The schedule** The architect said it 'should' take about six months. Now you have more detail you need to check with builders and suppliers to see what timescales they can meet.
- **The cost** The architect said it 'should' be about £100,000. Now you have more detail you need to check with builders and suppliers to see what their prices will be.
- **Managing and controlling the work** The architect might the right person to oversee the work, but it could be inappropriate for him/her to directly instruct the builders' and suppliers' workers. So a relationship between the architect and these teams needs to be established.

This analogy compares with MSP:

- You are the client you will pay for the work. In this sense you are more like the SRO.
- You and your family will live in this renovated house. It will transform your life. Here you are like business operations, and more equivalent to the BCM.
- The architect is similar to the programme manager.
- The builders and suppliers equate to the projects in the programme.

4.2 WHAT DOES MSP HAVE TO SAY?

The following sections are brief extracts from MSP that outline what the main guide says on the topic.

4.2.1 Vision

A vision is a picture of a better future; it is the basis for the outcomes and delivered benefits of the programme. As such it is a vital focus and enabler for the buy-in, motivation and activity alignment of the large community of people involved in any programme.

The vision statement is used to communicate the end goal of the programme, being a summary impression of the desired future state.

Characteristics of a good vision statement can be summarized as follows:

- It is written as a future state. It is not to be confused with an objective, strategy, intention or mission, all of which could begin with the word 'to'. Instead, it is a snapshot of the organization in the future.
- It can be easily understood by a wide variety of stakeholders; it is easy to communicate. This means it does not use jargon understood by only one group. It is clear in the vision statement how this better future is different from the present.
- It is written with the broadest groupings of stakeholders as the target audience.

- It describes a compelling future that engages the heart as well as the head. This does not mean it is emotional, but nor is it dry and factual.
- It sets out the current reality as part of the justification for the change – that is, why the organization cannot stay where it is.
- It matches the degree of transformation change with the boldness of the vision conveyed. Vision statements should motivate everyone and need to do justice to the challenge of transformational change.
- It avoids target dates unless the vision is truly time dependent.
- It describes a desirable future, in terms of the interests of key stakeholders. Key benefits are implicit.
- It describes a vision that is verifiable but without too many detailed performance targets. A vision statement that contains an inspirational future that is not verifiable can breed scepticism among stakeholders. It should be clear when the organization has arrived at the future state.
- It is sufficiently flexible to remain relevant over the life of the programme. It does not contain too many constraints.
- It provides sufficient context and direction to enable the development of the blueprint.

The statement needs to be short and memorable but relevant. Some of the best vision statements are no more than a few words long.

The vision underpins communications, and is communicated repeatedly at all kinds of events. Ideally, stakeholders should be able to recall it from memory almost word for word.

4.2.2 Blueprint

The programme's vision provides a description of the desired outcomes in customer-focused terms. As the vision is a description at a summary level it needs to be expanded and developed into a blueprint, which evolves and is refined during the lifecycle of the programme. It is the blueprint that provides a basis for modelling benefits and designing the projects dossier. Figure 4.2 shows how the MSP design documents fit together.

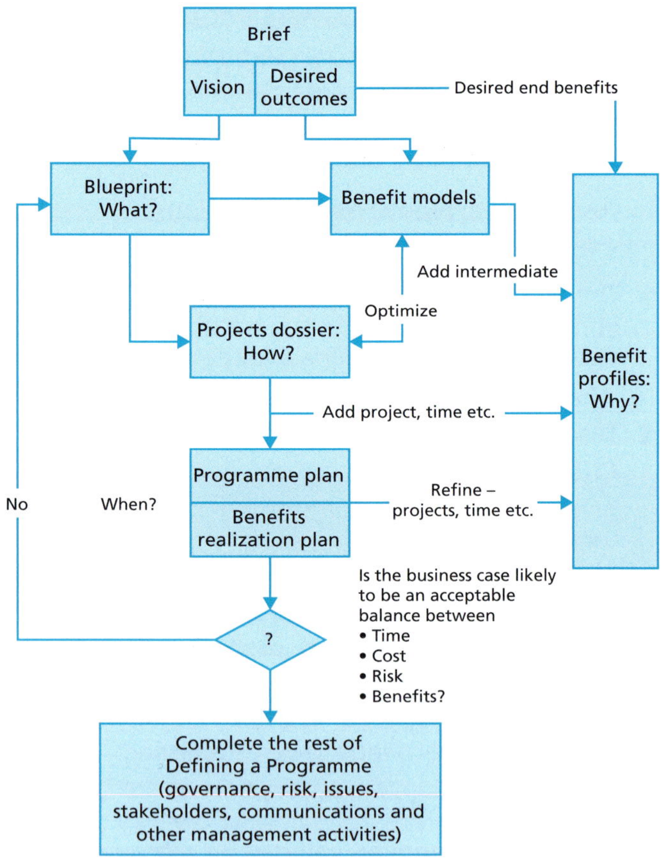

Figure 4.2 MSP design documents

The blueprint is not concerned with how to get to the future state. The 'how' is dealt with when designing the projects dossier. A number of scenarios will be considered for the final outcome of the programme along with the options for delivering these scenarios. The optimum outcomes and options for delivering these outcomes are selected. This is reviewed over the programme lifecycle to ensure they remain optimal.

The new capability occurs when the outputs from projects are put into operational use; once transition is completed the outcomes have been achieved and benefits can be realized.

The programme manager is responsible for organizing activities to ensure the blueprint is appropriately authored and owned. Where the programme manager and BCM have suitable skills and experience, they can be the authors of the blueprint. Where they don't, it is the responsibility of the programme manager, assisted by the BCM, to engage appropriately skilled people as authors.

The process, organization, tools and information (POTI) model sets a high-level scope of what must be included and integrated in an effective blueprint:

- **P** Processes, business models of operations and functions including operational costs and performance levels
- **O** Organizational structure, staffing levels, roles, skills requirements, organizational culture, supply chain and style
- **T** Technology, buildings, IT systems and tools, equipment, machinery and accommodation
- **I** Information and data required for the future business operations and performance measurement.

Each programme has to plan and manage the journey from the current operating model to the future operating model as described in the vision statement. An understanding of the current state and the gap (the difference between current and future states) is essential to be able to effectively explore alternative approaches to delivering the new capability.

The initial analysis of the gap is a comparison between the current organization (described in the current state section of the blueprint) and the design for the future organization (described in the future state section of the blueprint).

Elements of the blueprint, such as processes, technology etc., are compared as they are now with how they need to be. More detailed analysis will be carried out by projects, but there should be enough detail in the blueprint to be able to provide the business requirements for the projects.

4.3 WHAT DOES THIS MEAN TO YOU?

> *'Without leaps of imagination, or dreaming, we lose the excitement of possibilities. Dreaming, after all, is a form of planning.'* Gloria Steinem

You are the programme manager. That does not mean you are an expert at organization design. You also cannot be expected to have detailed knowledge of the operations that are going to be changed. Your role is to understand the process that needs to be followed then engage and oversee the work of those who do have the expertise and knowledge. These are some of the roles that you should consider involving. They may have different titles where you are working.

- **BCMs** They will be more knowledgeable and expert about the management and state of the operational part of the organization that are to be changed.

- **Business architects, process engineers, business analysts** Those who can analyse the current organization and design a better future organization. They may use methods such as Six Sigma, TOGAF etc.
- **Systems analysts, engineers, architects** Those who can design and appraise technical systems to underpin the future ways of working.
- **Building architects, facilities managers** Those who can design the facilities that the future organization will need.

The summary information about the projects that will be required is stored in a document called the projects dossier, which you are responsible for. You can't work out what projects you will need without a blueprint.

It is important that you facilitate the process of developing a blueprint so that it is in sufficient detail to allow you to commission and brief projects to deliver the required capabilities with adequate integrity of design interface.

As such, it is often easier to put the task on the back burner and get on with something more urgent. The problem with that is it never gets done, which means there is no clarity about what the projects need to deliver or where and how the benefits will materialize.

There are a number of fundamental reasons why blueprints don't get written. These can be summarized as:

- Inexperience of the programme team and leadership, who do not understand the need for it
- Just-do-it approach to programme delivery – let's get busy and see where we end up
- Programmes being run by project people who have no experience or knowledge of business modelling or change
- Lack of clarity within the programme or the organization on where it is going, and the process of blueprinting asks too many difficult questions
- Assumption that someone has already done it and knows where you are going.

4.3.1 What do you need to do about the vision?

Programmes are big on the vision thing. They come in many shapes and forms and have varying degrees of success, but they can be put into these categories:

- **The to-do list** A list of things that need to happen to achieve something. Such visions tend to focus on the obvious and often lack longevity and come to a stop in the first year.
- **Mission statement** Some blunt statements which sound good are not really a foundation for a programme. These statements tend to define what will happen, rather than the direction or destination.
- **Management waffle** A few sentences that are vague enough so that key stakeholders can agree, but have little relevance to what needs to happen or nobody is really sure what they mean.
- **Sermon** This kind of vision goes on for quite a long time, makes lots of promises that can't be achieved or measured, but excites some people for some of the time. It provides something for everyone but very little for most.
- **Rich pictures** These are quite often innovative and expensive. They can be very good at explaining the vision and the journey, though

Figure 4.3 Example of a rich picture

they can also sometimes be quite obscure and a bit cryptic. Figure 4.3 is an example of a rich picture from the London councils and illustrates the intended collaboration between different public bodies to improve services.

The majority of vision statements aren't really fit for the job. If anything they are a tick in a box to get the programme moving rather than focusing on the end game, and very few provide the basis for a blueprint. So here are a few tips on how to pull together a decent vision statement that has longevity.

Gather together the following information on which to build the vision statement:

- Drivers and justification for the programme
- Type of programme – compliance, vision-led or emergent?
- 'Must do' outcomes and any deadlines
- Services that will be changed, stopped or started
- Structural changes to the organization, market and supply chain
- Technology, infrastructure, legislation or property changes that are anticipated
- Values which need to be included that are close to the organization's heart (e.g. environmental sustainability).

Creating the statement will depend on the organizatiown, but don't be scared to make a few strong statements that stand alone. That is often easier than crafting a page of words. A statement on each of the above setting a positive, ambitious position would be a good start.

To test whether you have done a decent job, use the following checklist:

- Will it make sense to the stakeholders it is intended for?

- Does it clarify the current reality and justification for change?
- Will it survive changes of scope and timescales?
- Can you develop a blueprint from it?
- Will it act as the beacon and underpin decision-making?

Example

A great vision statement came from a director in the UK National Health Service (NHS). After listening to the principles of MSP and realizing that the first job was to sort out the vision, she said, 'Well, we've got to do it, so we had better mop up all the other things that are going on and do the best for the community while we are at it.' In one line she has recognized that they have a compliance programme, which had an element of 'emergent' in it, and then she set out a vision beyond both compliance and emergent.

4.3.2 What do you need to do about the blueprint?

Developing the blueprint is specialist work: your role is to help make it happen. Business architects are specialists in developing these models. Professional support in this area will be invaluable. Figure 4.4 illustrates how a blueprint might be constructed.

MSP Survival Guide for Business Change Managers provides a more detailed explanation of the role of business architects, and illustrations of how they might approach the business analysis. Remember that you are the custodian of the blueprint, not the BCMs or the business architect.

For specification-led programmes there is a temptation to focus totally on the structure, digging the tunnel or building the technology. This isn't surprising as this is where the money will be spent; however, the focus needs to be on how it will be managed and where the benefits will come from.

Business transformation programmes would focus on process and supply chain re-design so there is clarity about the end game. There may be some ambiguity but the options need to be identified and tracked.

Socio-economic programmes need to define the behaviour and structural changes that will be required as well as the infrastructure that must be put into place to support it.

Hints and tips

Imagine you are sailing a boat: the vision is your bow pointing at the horizon, but you need more to know how to get to and what to do at the destination. In a programme these are the blueprint, strategies and plans.

The blueprint contains key sets of information upon which the programme design and delivery will be based:

- **The 'as-is' state** How the parts of the organization that will be changed work at present.
- **The 'to-be' state** How the organization will work when the programme has completed.
- **Intermediate states** How the organization will be working at major control points (tranches in the MSP guide) during the lifecycle of the programme.

The blueprint itself can be constructed in a number of ways, using organization charts, flowcharts, process diagrams, soft systems mapping, technical diagrams covering buildings, IT, information flows and so on.

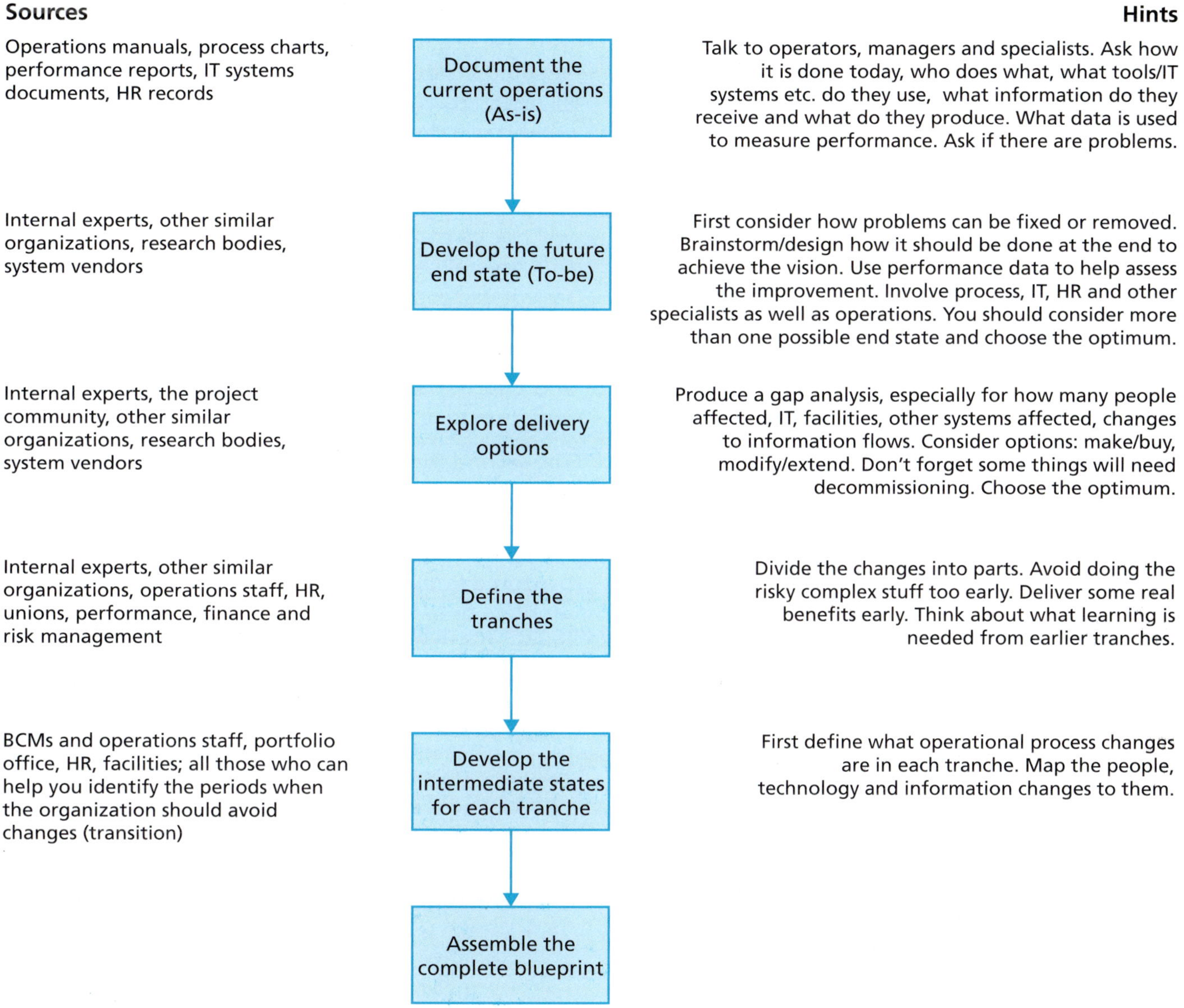

Figure 4.4 Example of the blueprint process

A programme is a long journey. When planning any journey there are some critical fundamentals:

- Where are you starting from (the 'as-is' state)?
- Where is journey's end, and how will we know when we have arrived (the 'to-be' final state)?
- It's a long journey so where do you need to stop en route and for what – fuel, drink, food? These stops are like the intermediate states.
- Could you complete a journey without this? No, of course you couldn't, so don't expect a programme to be any different.

One of the problems is to know where to start with the blueprint, as potentially it is a large document, highly complex and technical. Often the best starting point is to understand the current organization, or the part that is relevant to the scope of your programme. There are several reasons for this:

- Unless you are creating a brand-new organization or new function in the organization, you need to understand if there are parts of current operations that are broken. Building on malfunctioning operations is not a good idea.
- This will help you discover who needs to be involved. Start by talking to those who manage and run current operations. Ask them who they talk to when things go wrong or if they need to make minor changes. You start to understand what specialist skills are involved.
- People will have different opinions about the current state of this part of the organization. Carrying out a structured analysis will help to gain an objective assessment of what is in place and remove some of the subjectivity.
- You will probably do this via the BCM(s) who are close to the current operations. You will start to develop a critical relationship with another key MSP role.

Don't make the mistake of thinking that the POTI (process, organization, tools and information) are heading boxes into which to feed information. It is all driven by what the organization does now and what it will do in the future, so there must be clarity about how the elements fit together.

The first thing to remember is that the blueprint will not be created overnight and it is most likely that several people will need to be dedicated to the task: it will evolve as the programme understanding develops. Creating a blueprint may require specialist skills and knowledge: for example, enterprise design and business analysis skills rather than programme and change management skills.

The second thing to remember is confidentiality. While there will be much enthusiasm about developing and communicating the vision, the reality and detail of what is being planned will be stored in the blueprint with potentially much sensitive detail about structures, markets and other information that you may not wish to be communicated.

Example

When a programme brief for an Australian government department was reviewed, it turned out the programme team had not done a good job of outlining a detailed set of outcomes for the programme when presenting them to the sponsoring group. The sponsoring group had rejected them and said they wanted something different. What had happened was the team had presented the future very clearly, but in such a way that avoided the difficult issues: they were blaming the MSP approach rather than accepting the fact they didn't want to make difficult decisions.

If the programme needs to change multiple parts of the organization, multiple blueprints might be required. These should be in a common format so that they can be overlaid and compared at a later date. If they are written differently they will be incompatible and then be a waste of time. The aim is for a single blueprint document for the programme and there is a real need for pragmatism. The blueprint is likely to be constructed from a mix of formats ranging from flow diagrams to description documents.

Once the blueprint has been developed it will almost certainly evolve, but this must be controlled, as changes to the blueprint will affect the projects and the potential benefits. As well as being a design document, you should regard the blueprint as a control document. It defines the scope of the programme. Changes to it should be subject to change control, otherwise scope creep is likely. Change control procedures will be part of the issue management strategy – something you are responsible for.

4.3.2.1 How does it work now?

The POTI scope from MSP is very useful, but it isn't always the best place to start: very few organizations really know what their processes are. Despite all the rhetoric, most organizations depend on people's behaviour and what they need to get done rather than the processes they are supposed to follow.

The starting point is to ask the question 'What is it that we do now and how is it done?', which is the 'as-is' state in the blueprint.

It is surprising what will come out of this, but it will be in a language that everyone understands rather than technical terms that turn people off. The right people need to be involved: they must be the ones who know how things work now – in reality not theoretically.

4.3.2.2 How will it work in the future?

The challenge in producing the future state is that the vision statement may not be specific enough or adequate to enable this to happen. A vision statement is often a compromise that has been agreed to by all parties because they can interpret it differently for their own audiences: consequently, it becomes management waffle.

Dealing with management waffle or a vision statement that has managed to avoid any clear statements of intent is going to be a bit tricky, and this is the problem many programmes have when it comes to constructing the blueprint.

The advice on putting the blueprint together now applies to the future state, so the starting point is to ask the following questions:

- What services will be changed, stopped or started?
- What will be the impact of this on the way you operate?
- What structural changes to the organization, market and the supply chain will be required?
- What technology, infrastructure, legislation or property changes are anticipated?
- What information will you need to manage this and where will it come from?

4.3.2.3 What challenges will you face?

There are a number of challenges that you will face during the development of the blueprint. These can be regarded as risks for the programme and you may wish to have them logged formally so that they are visible to everyone.

Many organizations have found that they do have blueprint information, but it is dispersed around a number of documents. During the investigation it often comes to light that work has already taken place to develop some aspect of the blueprint and it is gathering dust somewhere or is embedded in disparate places, so part of this work is sniffing the information out and assembling it. The strategic business plan is often a good place to start, as the programme is almost certainly linked to a strategic objective of some sort.

Example

Some early blueprint work with a programme that had become a little becalmed happened to unearth the organization's three-year business plan. The document was a very aspirational and optimistic view of what their world would be like in three years' time, as expressed by each of the directors. It wasn't anything like a plan, but it was a very detailed vision statement that provided a good starting point for developing the blueprint.

So the challenges that you will face include:

- Dealing with those who just want to get on with it; there is now a brief so we know what needs to be done – let's start projects X, Y and Z. Further into the programme you are likely to discover that these projects are delivering the wrong things and it is now expensive to correct that mistake.
- Difficulty in finding people who know how systems actually work.
- Gaps between how they should work and how they do work.
- Getting decisions made about the level of change that is acceptable.
- Conflicting priorities from different groups leading to different requirements.
- Disagreements between BCMs on the way forward.
- Lack of strategic commitment to the level of necessary change.
- Existing projects that are not aligned with what is needed but nobody has the will to stop them.
- Finding the right resources and expertise to do the work.
- Confidentiality: some of the issues that arise may be very sensitive, particularly in terms of industrial relations and the press.

Some ideas on how these problems can be addressed:

- Organize briefing sessions to explain what a blueprint is, why it is important, and the process the programme will follow for its design and management.
- Use workshops to get people involved, but ensure they are properly briefed.
- Set up targeted questionnaires to gather views and details on how things currently function and how they could be improved.
- Introduce quality management systems.
- Use existing strategies that set out how things may work, for example, ICT or property.
- Use handbooks and guidelines that explain how operations work.

Enterprise architecture is now a well-developed concept which is complementary to the blueprint in MSP. It is too big a topic to cover in this publication but an internet search is always a good starting point to find out more.

Hints and tips

Strategy is executed by managers who own business processes that are run by operators using systems that are supported by IT or machines which process information or materials that are moved and stored via communication systems, transport and buildings.

Business modelling techniques such as Six Sigma, TOGAF[1] and OBASHI[2] may all have a potential role to play in the development of your blueprint.

An alternative view of business architecture is shown in Figure 4.5.

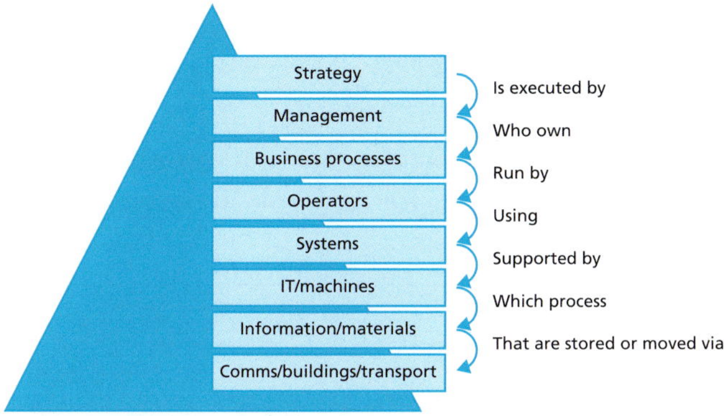

Figure 4.5 An alternative view of business architecture structure

4.3.3 What happens if you don't have a blueprint?

The consequences of not having a blueprint are often not immediately apparent to a programme. Hopefully there will be a vision and the programme will set off launching projects that will provide the energy to take them to the perceived destination. This happy state can last for up to a year – sometimes more. The organization will be pleased about the apparent progress and the programme team will be motivated and energized, delivering projects and reporting on their progress.

The problems begin to emerge between six and 12 months into the programme. The programme will appear disengaged from the organization that it is changing, because it has little understanding of the organization that it is planning to change. The programme board will be focused on project delivery, and if it did manage to appoint business change managers their role would be rather vague and ambiguous.

Decision-making which was fast and energetic in the early days will become slower; problems will become more complex with priorities and the basis for decisions being unclear; momentum will be lost and the programme will appear to become becalmed.

This is not necessarily a disaster, as it is a chance to regroup, consider where the programme is going and put the appropriate controls in place. Many programmes experience this; using the MSP framework as a point of reference, in reality the programme has achieved the first step change in capability, as it has realized that delivering a programme through project techniques and lots of energy isn't enough.

This isn't always the case; some programmes that are short term (often compliance programmes) with big targets to hit and hard deadlines can be successful in forcing a change through. The test of whether it was a true programme is whether the change sticks and the benefits come from the investment.

[1] TOGAF® is the de facto global standard for enterprise architecture (see http://www.opengroup.org/subjectareas/enterprise/togaf).

[2] The OBASHI methodology was developed to document, map and model how people, process and technology make a business work (see http://obashi.co.uk).

4.4 YOUR ROLE IN DEVELOPING THE VISION AND BLUEPRINT

In summary, here are the key things to think about.

4.4.1 Programme manager

The programme manager has responsibility for the actual blueprint document, as it is a core part of the programme controls: the projects will be initiated to create the capability that is described in the blueprint. Therefore, if the blueprint does not exist or is incomplete then the wrong projects may be launched. The programme manager should be pushing to get the job done and provide help and experience where appropriate; the content must be owned by the BCMs.

While you are not expected to be the author of the blueprint, you should take the view that it is your responsibility to get it written by the right people. You can therefore play a key role in identifying the people with the right skills and experience, forming them into an effective blueprint design team, and assisting with planning/managing the work.

4.4.2 Business change manager

The BCM is not alone in undertaking this work but the result of the work is going to shape your role for the life of the programme and the destiny of the organization.

You will need to work closely with the BCMs: conflicts are inevitable over the structure of the future organization, which may shape people's power bases once the programme is over and will colour their contributions. If the problems cannot be resolved at the programme board then the sponsoring group will need to be engaged.

4.4.3 Senior responsible owner

Ultimately, the SRO is accountable for what the programme produces and must sign off the blueprint. As such, they should be heavily engaged in the process, providing advice and direction to resolve strategic or tactical issues quickly. The SRO is also the conduit to the sponsoring group and should refer any conflicts that cannot be resolved upwards accordingly.

Table 4.1 is from the MSP guide and sets out the specific areas of focus for each role in developing the vision and blueprint.

Table 4.1 Areas of focus for the key roles in blueprint design and delivery

Role	Area of focus
Senior responsible owner (SRO)	Providing strategic direction for the work of the design of the blueprint and analysis of delivery options
	Ensuring sponsoring group authorization and commitment to the 'to-be' state, demonstrated through active cooperation; for example, making appropriate resource available to assist with the design of the blueprint and analysis of delivery options
	Ensuring that the blueprint document remains aligned with the strategic direction of the organization and will promote a coherent capability
	Providing the interface to the sponsoring group and other key stakeholders, maintaining their buy-in; for example, as the design of the future organization becomes clearer
	Providing advice and direction to the programme manager and BCM(s) as required, including risks or issues identified during blueprint design and delivery
	Ensuring that the programme board assesses and understands the implications of the blueprint and its delivery
Programme manager	Ensuring that the blueprint document is authored and assembled in collaboration with the BCM(s)
	Working closely with the BCM(s) to ensure that the blueprint, programme plan, benefits realization plan and benefit profiles are consistent and able to deliver the business case
	Ensuring the programme has access to competent resources to create the blueprint
	Ensuring that appropriate options appraisals to select the optimal 'to-be' state take place
	Ensuring that the management of changes is undertaken with an impact assessment on the blueprint
	Communicating the details of the blueprint to the relevant projects and other programmes
	Ensuring that the planned step changes in operational capability are clearly understood by the project teams
	Ensuring that uncertainties and ambiguities relating to the content of the blueprint are captured as risks
	Contributing to managing stakeholder expectations

Table continues

Table 4.1 *continued*

Role	Area of focus
Business change manager(s)	Leading the development of the content and taking responsibility for the delivery of the design into business operations Consulting with and gaining support from senior business managers for the 'to-be' state Ensuring that the planned step changes in operational capability are clearly understood by the operational areas Providing and coordinating essential input to the blueprint with the assistance of experienced operational staff and specialists, and (where appropriate) authoring (at least part of) the blueprint Ensuring that 'as-is' and 'to-be' information from the blueprint is used to construct the benefit profiles Aligning the creation of the capability within the blueprint with benefits realization through approval of project outputs Ensuring that operational changes during the life of the programme are being reflected in the evolving 'as-is' state in the blueprint
Programme office	Providing or locating information and resources that can assist with the design of the blueprint Facilitating impact assessments of changes on the blueprint Maintaining configuration control of the blueprint

5

Benefits management

5 Benefits management

'There is nothing more difficult to take in hand, more perilous to conduct, or more uncertain in its success, than to take the lead in the introduction of a new order of things.'
Niccolò Machiavelli

For you as the programme manager this is an important part of your day job. Your role exists to deliver capability that will enable change, either internally or externally of the organization. The justification for this change is the achievement of strategic objective through the realization of benefits.

Research by KPMG in 2006 suggested that less than 80% of predicted benefits were delivered in the average project. Analysis of the result of the P3M3 maturity assessments in 2012 by Aspire Europe showed that 81% of organizations were at level 1 maturity for benefits management, which means that there were no formal processes or plans in place to deliver benefits for the vast majority of initiatives, which in effect supported the conclusions of KPMG and showed that little had changed in the six years in between.

The reality of the situation is that most investments and programmes do achieve positive results but do not produce a good return on the investment. The problem is that programmes do not focus enough on benefits, doing little to track or record them, so there is no objective evidence about the scale of improvement. As a programme manager you should have more experience of benefits management than most BCMs. So you are going to change all that!

Benefits management is largely the domain of the BCM, and as such, it is covered in much more depth in the *MSP Survival Guide for Business Change Managers*.

5.1 BASIC PRINCIPLES

Benefits are the positive effects of change. Within the programme the change that is required is the difference between the current state and future state as defined in the blueprint. Therefore there is an inherent link between the blueprint and the benefits.

The blueprint describes what the current state is and what the future state will be. Further design (e.g. projects dossier) and analysis (e.g. benefits map) will define the benefits that will result from the change. So if insufficient effort is invested in developing a detailed understanding for the blueprint, then the basis for estimating benefits will be flawed and, in effect, the benefits will be guesswork – and in most cases, bad guesses.

Example

An IT call centre rationalization included a number of upgrade projects which were needed but were difficult to justify. By raising the bar and combining them as a programme with a more ambitious rationalization of the processes and structures based on the combined effect of the new technology, the programme business case was much easier to sell.

Figure 5.1 shows how the achievement of intermediate states in the blueprint can give the opportunity to release and measure benefits.

The problem with programmes is that they tend to put all their focus on the cost of creating the change rather than the beneficial effects of the change.

The type of programme will significantly affect the approach to benefits.

5.1.1 Guiding principles

Here are the guiding principles for effective benefits management (for more detail, see *MSP Survival Guide for Business Change Managers*):

- Establish the guiding mind (a senior manager maintaining the focus)
- Create a transparent and tangible evidence base
- Allocate attribution for achievement (who benefits?)

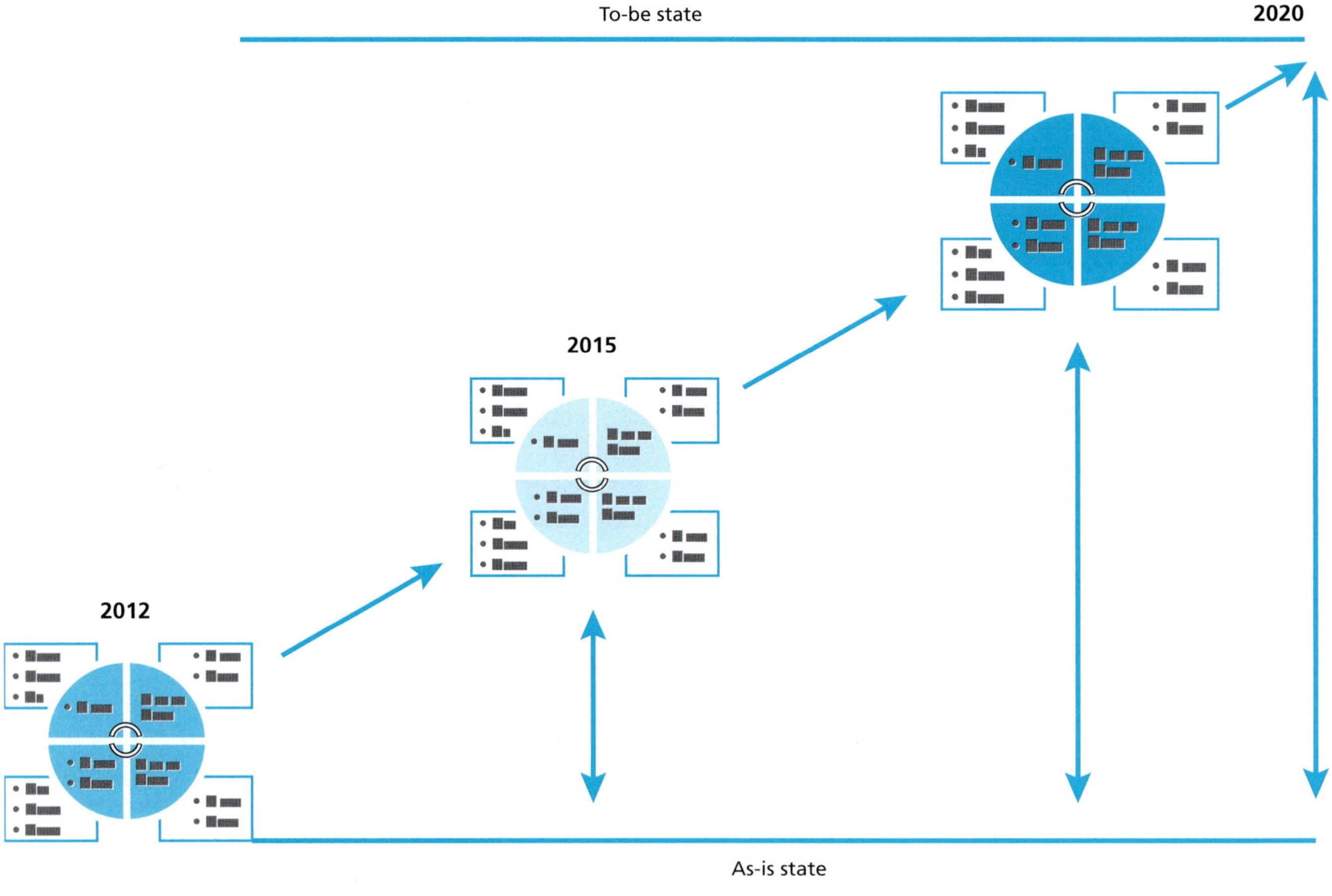

Figure 5.1 Programme intermediate states

- Conduct a risk-based valuation
- Maintain control of change
- Ensure consistent valuations.

For example, numeric levels could be applied to individual benefits as follows:

- Low risk = 90% of the value is achievable
- Medium risk = 60% of the value is achievable
- High risk = 30% of the value is achievable.

> *'Nothing defines humans better than their willingness to do irrational things in the pursuit of phenomenally unlikely payoffs.'* Scott Adams

5.2 WHAT DOES MSP HAVE TO SAY?

Benefits management is at the very heart of programme management: programmes are primarily driven by the need to deliver benefits. This is achieved by the programme's projects creating outputs, which build capabilities, which in turn transition into outcomes that serve the purpose of realizing benefits for the organization. However, it is likely that the programme will have some negative impacts as well as improvements.

Where a negative effect of the change can be forecast, then this is termed a dis-benefit. Benefits and dis-benefits can be defined as follows:

- A **benefit** is the measurable improvement resulting from an outcome perceived as an advantage by one or more stakeholders, which contributes towards one or more organizational objective(s).
- A **dis-benefit** is the measurable decline resulting from an outcome perceived as negative by one or more stakeholders, which detracts from one or more organizational objective(s).

Understanding the differences and relationships between outputs, capabilities, outcomes and benefits is key to understanding benefits management (see Table 5.1).

Given its importance to the programme, it is not surprising that benefits management drives many aspects of programme management including:

- Aligning and validating the integrity of the blueprint against the projects, activities and associated organizational changes needed to deliver the new capabilities and benefits
- Defining the aggregate of achieved benefits, expected benefits, costs to date and expected cost against the business case; providing a crucial test of the ongoing viability of the programme
- Prioritizing benefits to allow the programme to create maximum value under given constraints and make the right trade-off decisions if required
- Planning the programme (benefits realization is a major foundation for this aspect)
- Engaging with stakeholders to understand impact and helping win support
- Defining what is a fit-for-purpose capability, establishing what the critical quality-checking mechanisms throughout the programme would be and checking that they are aligned with the requirements in the blueprint
- Informing end-of-tranche reviews to enable decisions on changes to the programme going forward and underlying governance to be made
- Ensuring that the costs associated with Delivering the Capability are balanced with the value of the benefits in the business case
- Monitoring the risks and issues that may impact benefits realization.

Table 5.1 Differences between outputs, capabilities, outcomes and benefits

	Output	Capability	Outcome	Benefit
Description	The deliverable, or output developed by a project from a planned activity	The completed set of project outputs required to deliver an outcome; exists prior to transition	A new operational state achieved after transition of the capability into live operations	The measurable improvement resulting from an outcome perceived as an advantage by one or more stakeholders and which contributes towards one or more organizational objective(s)
Rationale	Answers at least in part the fundamental question 'What do you need to create to enable the change?'	Answers the question 'What will you need to have in place to enable the new operating state?'	Answers the question 'What is the desired operational state of the organization using these new things?'	Answers the question 'Why is this justified?' (i.e. it explains what a programme delivers)
Example	An individual component of an e-commerce system, application, hardware, new business processes training etc.	An e-commerce system tested and ready to go into operation and with trained staff	Transformed client service organization, faster processing, fulfilling and charging for web-based orders	Increased sales revenues of x%

5.2.1 Benefits categorization

Categorizing benefits can help organizations to better model their priorities and planning and ensure that there is a balanced portfolio of benefits. By categorizing benefits effectively, organizations are able to:

- Balance the mix of benefits that are being sought and the associated risk profiles
- Enable effective reporting and tracking by category
- Identify potential overlaps of benefit counting
- Understand the impact of changes on different parts of the organization
- Track the relationship between objectives and benefits
- Help to manage changes to priorities within the programmes. If there is a strategic change in the value types being sought, the programme will be more agile in its ability to see the impact across the programme
- Help to create a common set of terminology for referring to benefits and bring greater transparency
- Enable a portfolio-level view of benefits across programmes and projects through consistency.

There are many different ways to categorize benefits. The following benefit categories are well established, but they are not exhaustive:

- Value
- Financial impact
- Corporate objective
- Stakeholder impact
- Timeline
- Levels of risk.

5.3 WHAT DOES THIS MEAN TO YOU?

> *'If you want to make enemies, try to change something.'* Woodrow Wilson

Within the main MSP guide everything to do with benefits tracks back to the BCM, because the BCM is the organization's face within the programme structure and, as such, within the MSP framework they are personally responsible.

Remember that in many programmes the outputs from more than one project are needed to provide the future capability required. You should expect to spend considerable time coordinating and facilitating groups of people who have different perspectives, expertise and knowledge. Unreasonable assumptions and misunderstanding are commonplace in the early parts of many programmes. If you don't scrutinize the work of these people carefully significant issues can arise later in the programme and will then be expensive to fix. How often have you heard this as projects are about to deliver their products: 'That isn't right!' 'But it's what you asked for ...' 'But it's not what we wanted!'

You will need to contribute to a number of documents that detail what benefits will be delivered, where and how this will happen. There is a brief description of each in Appendix A of the main MSP guide and what your role should be.

The benefits strategy sets out the framework within which the programme will operate and deliver benefits (see Figure 5.2).

The benefit profiles are the detailed descriptions of how each benefit will be achieved and measured. You don't want too many of these and it is better to have a small number of well-defined benefits than many diverse and poorly understood benefits.

The benefits realization plans are the tracking devices to ensure your benefits appear and that they are proven and signed off.

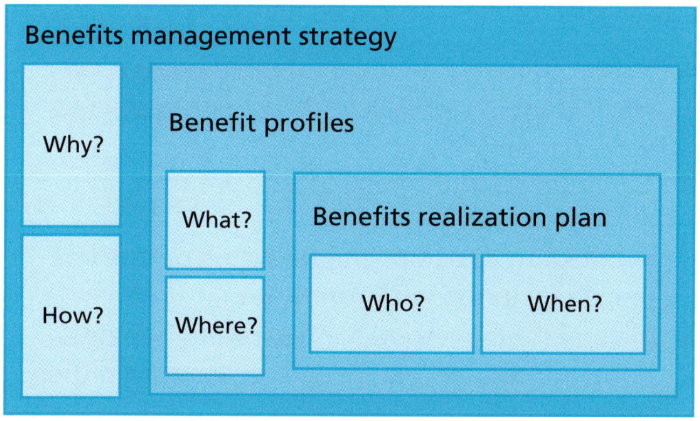

Figure 5.2 Benefits theme documentation

5.3.1 Benefits management cycle

> *'Where is the knowledge we have lost in information?'* T. S. Eliot, *Choruses from the Rock*

As with most of the themes there is a cycle of activities that run throughout the programme. It is your job to manage this cycle and ensure that it happens.

There are four steps that cover the evolution of benefits and their maintenance.

There is a detailed explanation of the sources of benefits and how to manage the cycle in the *MSP Survival Guide for Business Change Managers*: this directly relates to business performance, which is primarily their part of the programme.

5.3.2 Benefits management strategy

'If you can't measure it, you can't manage it, and if you can't manage it then it isn't a benefit.'

Even though most of the work and content comes from the BCMs, you are responsible for governance so you need to produce the benefits management strategy. In Chapter 2 we outlined the core elements of each of the strategies and this section provides advice specifically on benefits controls:

- Ensure there is a single guiding mind that can arbitrate on how to evaluate benefits and avoid double-counting.
- Common measurement criteria are needed to evaluate benefits, e.g. the value of a death avoided on a road or the full value of one less employee in the workforce.
- Include some method for risk-rating benefits: none are certain and many are less certain than others.
- Include a method for pinpointing where the benefit will be visible, so that there will be tangible evidence of the change.
- Define how project or operational changes will be tracked: this is a common source of benefits evaporation.
- Define where and how actions to release benefits will be managed and who is accountable.
- Define the types of benefits the organization is chasing – producing happy staff when you were supposed to save money won't get you very far.
- Specify what indicators will be monitored for evidence of benefits achievement and how the data will be sourced, and by whom.
- Make sure everyone understands the difference between benefits, outcomes, capability and outputs; if you do not, it will haunt you at every meeting.
- How will benefits management-related activities be funded?
- How will validation and sign-off of benefits be managed?

Well-designed templates can help, but all programmes are unique and your benefit management strategy will define the information needed to manage your programme's benefits.

5.3.3 Benefits management procedure

This is a summary of typical benefits management activities. Most of this is done by the BCMs but you need to make sure it is done well, and perhaps use your planning and control expertise in support (see Figure 5.3 for an example):

- Identify benefits
- Determine measures
- Map to outputs, capabilities and outcomes
- Determine the timeline (programme plan and benefits realization plan)
- Monitor pre-transition (based on project artefacts); look for opportunities to get more benefits
- Measure post-transition; look for opportunities to get more benefits
- Review at the end of each tranche; lessons learned, improve for next tranche, use as input to plan the next tranche.

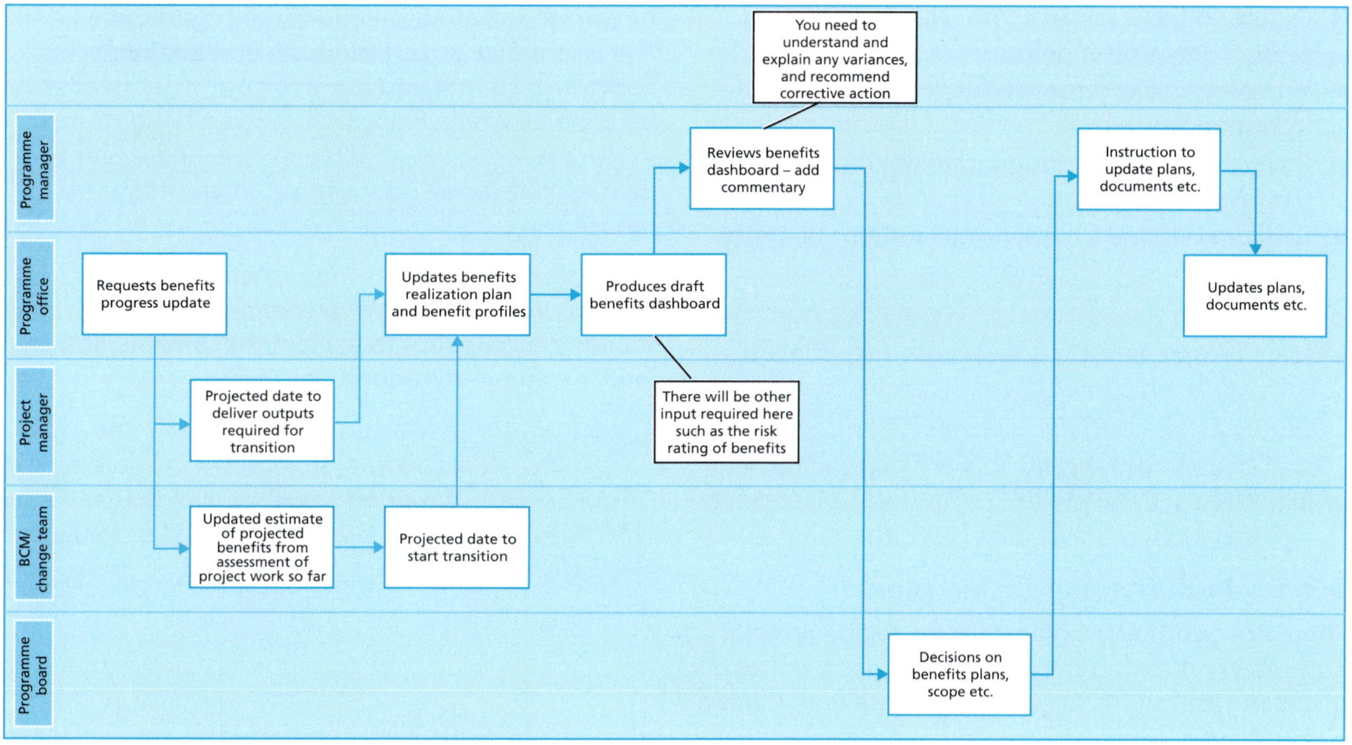

Figure 5.3 Example of the benefit monitoring process before transition

5.3.4 Challenges that you will face

There are a number of challenges you will face as the programme manager: hopefully the information and explanations provided will help to set you off in the right direction, but be prepared to deal with one or more of these:

- Capability of the BCM and the change teams
- Lack of a blueprint or very little information on where the benefits will come from
- Misunderstanding between the project teams and operations as to how the outputs relate to benefits
- Project culture where benefits are someone else's problem, and insufficient engagement between the project and operational people occurs through the specify, design and build phases
- Demands on your time for information to help justify the benefit claims
- Unreasonable expectations of what the potential benefits are
- Tendency of the SRO to want to get on with it and worry about benefits later
- Resistance of stakeholders and colleagues to being measured and excuses such as 'we don't have the data'

- Failure to focus on risks that will affect benefits rather than project delivery
- Unreasonable estimates based on poor-quality information
- Political pressure to exaggerate benefits to justify the investment
- Lack of skills and experience to support benefits.

Example

Aspire Europe maturity assessments over the last eight years show that 81% of organizations are at maturity level 1 (awareness or ad hoc) for benefits management, so the biggest challenge is often the maturity of the organization.

5.3.5 Benefits realization plan

There are two ways to plan. Start at the beginning and work forwards is the normal approach, but one of the problems is that the timing of the end doesn't fit with the strategic needs of the programme. The alternative is to start at the end and work backwards so that you can work out what needs to be done by when. Figure 5.4 shows a benefits map in reverse order, which some people find easier to deal with. It shows how a government might try to reduce costs.

The plan is key to illustrating where and when benefits will happen. We recommend you use something graphical to explain the timeline and improve communications.

Hints and tips

The BCM can be a great ally in achieving the benefits realization plan. Treat him/her as your best friend.

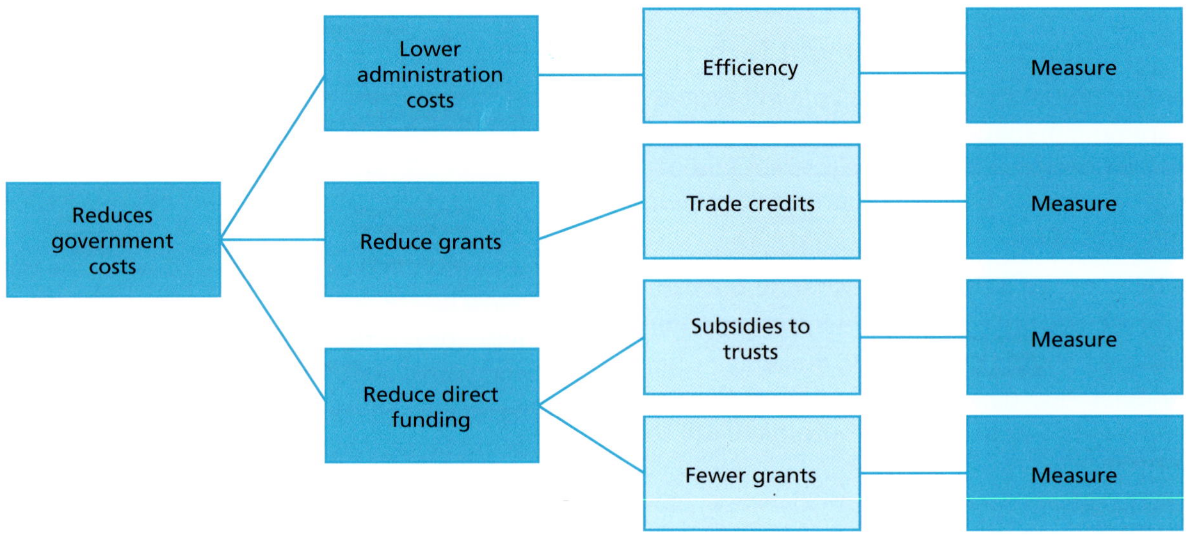

Figure 5.4 Example of a benefits map in reverse order

5.3.6 Benefits scrutiny and challenge

It is very important that benefits are differentiated from simply desirable things that the organization might want to do.

It is quite often the case that statements are made and included in documentation as benefits, when in fact they are outputs from projects and or outcomes resulting from changes being implemented.

To technically qualify as a benefit, the DOAM test as shown in Table 5.2 should be applied (see *MSP Survival Guide for Business Change Managers* for more detail on the DOAM test).

If you are unable to attribute or measure the benefit, then it is very likely that you are dealing with an outcome. That is not to say that you can't ever measure or attribute outcomes, but they can be less tangible: for example happier staff.

5.4 YOUR ROLE IN BENEFITS MANAGEMENT

You are the pivotal role in overseeing the projects that will deliver the means to enable the capabilities required to achieve the outcome and benefits. You need to have high visibility in the programme as the person responsible for enabling the changes that result in the benefits. It is common in many projects that their focus stretches no further than producing outputs that are fit for purpose. Project teams typically regard 'fit for purpose' as functioning correctly according to a specification. This can be a major flaw in a programme. A new process or system can function reliably but does not enable the scale of improvement in business operations that is needed to achieve the benefits. A critical part of your role is to ensure there is significant collaboration between the project teams and operational staff.

5.4.1 Business change managers

With the BCMs you will need to work closely together to establish that 'guiding mind' to ensure that there is a common approach to benefits (defined in the benefits management strategy). The benefit profiles and the detailed analysis that justifies the programme and defines the destination for your part of the organization, including ensuring that there is no double-counting of benefit, is a key part of justifying the programme. The flip side of this is that if the projects cannot produce enablers who will realize all the benefits, you are going

Table 5.2 DOAM test for benefits

Description	It should be clear from the description what the positive (or negative for a dis-benefit) effect of the change will be.
Observable outcomes	It should be possible to describe the changes that are required to realize the benefit, what outputs are required from projects, and the changes and subsequent outcomes that will need to be in place.
Attribution	It must be possible to attribute where in the organization improvement will be generated and who is responsible for ensuring it happens.
Measurement	If you can't measure it you can't manage it, and if you cannot manage it then it is unlikely to happen.

to need to be courageous and make the position clear. There may be some desired changes that are just too ambitious. Work with the BCMs to try to identify these as early as possible. But equally be prepared to offer alternative options that do justify an acceptable business case.

You will need to get the BCMs to sign off the projects to ensure they meet operational needs. You will also need to ensure that any issues and changes that arise during the project delivery don't undermine the blueprint and remove capabilities that future operations are reliant on. But don't think the BCMs are only involved at the end of the projects: they (or their representatives) need to work closely with projects throughout their lifecycles, to make sure requirements are clear, that projects are developing what operations will be able to use, and all of this will actually enable the benefits to be realized.

Hints and tips

Consider getting BCMs to sign off projects at key milestones such as brief, definition, specification, design, prototype and system testing, so they can be confident the project output will enable them to realize the operational improvements.

5.4.2 Senior responsible owner

The SRO will ultimately have their reputation on the line so benefits are going to be a very sensitive issue. In some circumstances the SRO will be open to acknowledging the difficulty with benefits as this will enable them to ensure the sponsoring group recognizes that the programme may still need to go ahead but can't be justified purely on benefits: for example, as in a compliance programme. In other circumstances the programme may be their personal mission, and as such lack of benefits may not be welcomed. Either way you will need to judge the political climate in your organization, but if the benefits don't appear and you say they will, guess who is going to get the blame?

5.4.3 Project teams

The project teams will need to engage regularly with the BCM and related roles such as the senior user. As well as making sure this happens you may need to help to ensure the project communicates in terms that operational people can understand. Consider the use of prototypes, story boards, use cases etc.

Table 5.3 shows the key roles in benefits management as given in the MSP guide.

Table 5.3 Areas of focus for the key roles in benefits management

Role	Area of focus
Senior responsible owner (SRO)	Reports to the sponsoring group on the delivery of the programme benefits as described in the benefit profiles
	Ensures that the programme and the business areas affected maintain a focus on benefits delivery
	Ensures that the benefits management strategy is created, adjusted, improved and enforced
	Maintains a focus on business performance sustainability during transition

Role	Area of focus
Senior responsible owner *continued*	Chairs benefit reviews involving relevant stakeholders, business managers and possibly internal audits Liaises with the sponsoring group on the validation of all benefits claimed by the programme Authorizes benefits achievements
Programme manager	Develops the benefits management strategy on behalf of the SRO with the BCMs and relevant stakeholders from the affected business areas Develops the benefits realization plans in consultation with the BCMs, relevant stakeholders and members of the project teams Ensures that the delivery of capability is aligned to maximize the realization of benefits Initiates benefit reviews as part of the benefits realization plans or in response to any other triggers
Business change manager(s)	Identifies and quantifies the benefits with the support of relevant stakeholders, the programme manager and members of the project teams Delivers particular benefits as profiled: this extends to ensuring that commitments and actions that have been attributed to operational areas are delivered Provides information to support the creation and delivery of the benefits realization plan Develops and maintains the benefit profiles Ensures there is no double-counting of benefits Maintains engagement with key individuals responsible for benefits delivery within the operations Sets business performance deviation levels and early-warning indicators to support realizing benefits Initiates benefit reviews after the programme has closed
Programme office	Monitors the progress of benefits realization against plan Gathers information for the benefit reviews Produces performance reports as defined by the programme manager Maintains benefits information under change control and maintains audit trails of changes

6 Leadership and stakeholder engagement

6 Leadership and stakeholder engagement

'It usually takes more than three weeks to prepare a good impromptu speech.' Mark Twain

The UK National Audit Office has concluded that stakeholder perception is one of the critical factors in whether a programme is a success or failure. There are numerous examples of successful programmes that have delivered their objectives and benefits yet were perceived as a failure, and vice versa: some badly run programmes have failed on all fronts, but were still perceived as a success.

As the programme manager you are going to play a critical role in stakeholder engagement. You are responsible for preparing, embedding and monitoring programme governance. The stakeholder engagement strategy and the communication plan are critical inputs to successful engagement. Your role also means you probably have the widest range of stakeholders to engage with. You work with the senior responsible owner (SRO), report to the programme board, collaborate with the business change managers (BCMs) and oversee all the projects.

MSP Survival Guide for Business Change Managers provides more information on the softer side and content of stakeholder and communications as they are gateways into the main stakeholder groups. This survival guide focuses more on the process, which is your area of responsibility.

6.1 BASIC PRINCIPLES

> **Hints and tips**
>
> Before gaining the confidence of others, you will need to gain confidence and belief in yourself.

There are plenty of books, courses and seminars on leadership so this section will concentrate on stakeholders and communications. The root of good practice in this area comes from marketing disciplines, and many of the techniques have evolved from there and been converted for use by programmes. The key principles are:

- **Leadership** It may sound obvious, but leaders have followers, so your role is to create followers for the programme vision within the programme and project team. At the programme board you may be the more junior, so may have less experience of leadership. This is fundamentally about building relationships with programme members and stakeholders (beyond the imposed contractual or organizational), providing them with direction (although not necessarily being responsible for identifying what that direction is, typically through ensuring that the blueprint is understood by all) and then ensuring that the team's efforts deliver the benefits. Simple principles, but often one or all of these factors is missing.

  Leadership is different for each person – not only in what they do but also how they do it. You will look to the SRO for leadership, while the programme team and projects will look to you.

- **Identifying and analysing stakeholders** The first thing you need to know is who they are and what they are interested in. It sounds a simple enough requirement, but when you start to dig into it, then it becomes complex and it is often underestimated. This is not creating a contact list that you can send a monthly email to and hope that people read it. You and the team will need to find a way of categorizing them and working out the best way to influence them; high-level groups such as 'staff' are of no use as they are too generic.

  Once you know who the stakeholders are and what you think they might be interested in you will need to know how interested they are, their attitude to your programme (positive or negative), and whether you are going to need things from them or you are going to be doing things to them – or both.
- **Communicating effectively** Once you have identified the stakeholders and understand what they want and don't want, you can target the communications much more effectively and achieve the results you need. Communication is two-way: it is not about you downloading information but about listening to the reactions, so you will need to put channels in place to deal with this.

Example

After completing the stakeholder session on a BCM course for one of the London councils, one of the senior managers said, 'Crikey, this is a lot of work, but we can either do it up front and maintain some sort of control, or leave it and spend lots of time fire-fighting and responding to challenges when we are in delivery – either way it is going to be a lot of hard work.'

6.2 WHAT DOES MSP HAVE TO SAY?

MSP defines a stakeholder as any individual, group or organization that can affect, be affected by, or perceives itself to be affected by a programme. There is an inherent link between leadership and stakeholders, which is manifested in the following ways:

- Leaders use the programme vision statement to influence and persuade stakeholders to commit to the beneficial future.
- Business change managers engage their operational stakeholders, leading them through the uncertainty of transition to the new ways of working.
- A focus on benefits recognizes that a 'benefit' is only such when it is perceived to be advantageous by one or more stakeholders. In a community of different interests and attitudes the leader must engage stakeholders so that benefits are identified, clearly communicated and understood, owned and realized, and the threats to realizing those benefits are reduced.
- Some stakeholders will be identified as resources within the delivery of the new capability – some with unique or scarce skills and competencies.

MSP provides advice and guidance on:

- The nature of stakeholder engagement and the need to evaluate and assess their impact and information needs from the programme.
- Defining leadership where this has impacts on how stakeholders are engaged and understood, including considering internal politics, individual emotions and motivations.
- Business change management in the wider context, where a programme may be seen as a part of a larger strategic change initiative or part of a corporate portfolio of change.

- Communications in the programme over and above project communications in line with an engagement strategy.

6.2.1 Programme communications plan

The programme communications plan describes what will be communicated, how it will be communicated, when, and by whom, during the programme. It should be designed and implemented as early as possible and then maintained throughout the programme.

Using information from the stakeholder profiles, the activities within the programme communications plan should be designed to:

- Raise awareness among all stakeholders of the benefits and impact of the planned outcomes.
- Gain commitment from stakeholders in the target business area(s) to the changes being introduced – thus ensuring the long-term success of the improvements.
- Keep all stakeholders in the target business area(s) informed of progress before, during and after implementation or delivery of programme outcomes.
- Promote key messages from the programme.
- Demonstrate a commitment to meeting the requirements of those sponsoring the programme (the sponsoring group).
- Make communications truly two-way (i.e. a dialogue, not a broadcast) by actively encouraging stakeholders to provide feedback and ensuring that they are informed about the use of their feedback to influence the programme. All types of feedback should be expected, and responses to it carefully considered. Feedback may sometimes be negative, impractical or harshly critical.
- Ensure that all those responsible for projects have an understanding of the scope, nature and outcomes of the programme.
- Promote outcomes to maximize the benefits obtained from the new business operations.

> **Hints and tips**
>
> Successful communications are based on four core elements (think 'SMEF'):
>
> - **Stakeholder identification and analysis** Send the right message to the right audience.
> - **Message clarity and consistency** Ensure relevance and recognition, and engender trust.
> - **Effective system of message delivery** Get the right messages to the right stakeholders in a timely and effective way.
> - **Feedback collection system** Assess the effectiveness of the communications process.

6.3 WHAT DOES THIS MEAN TO YOU?

'The degree of one's emotion varies inversely with one's knowledge of the facts – the less you know, the hotter you get.' Bertrand Russell

Stakeholder engagement can be difficult and hard work for the following reasons:

- It's about people. In a programme there are likely to be wide-ranging opinions, attitudes, and levels of understanding. Successful engagement means understanding and being sensitive to these factors.
- Some people see communications as getting in the way of getting on with the real job.
- When the going gets tough, communications are often one of the first types of activity to be dropped.

As programme manager you will set up the governance and infrastructure to enable stakeholder engagement, but that does not mean you do all the communicating: there will be others in a better position to be effective, either in the change or project teams.

The stakeholder management strategy sets out the framework within which the programme will operate and deliver stakeholder management (see Figure 2.2).

The stakeholder profiles are detailed descriptions about each stakeholder (including their interests and influences) and how the programme will engage with them.

The communications plans are the tracking devices to ensure your stakeholder engagement is managed effectively.

6.3.1 The stakeholder lifecycle and techniques

> *'Electric communication will never be a substitute for the face of someone who with their soul encourages another person to be brave and true.'* Charles Dickens

The same common cycle of activities that is found in the themes (see Figure 2.1) applies to stakeholders and communications.

The cycle is continuous and begins on day one of the programme. Stakeholder identification is needed to work out who is the sponsoring group, so it is behaviour as much as process.

It is certainly the case that stakeholder engagement comes naturally to some people, and these steps will help to put some structure around what they do naturally. For others it will be opening up a new world of complexity and intrigue.

You will set out the fundamentals; the rules, procedures, responsibilities, tools etc. in the stakeholder engagement strategy. You must make sure these are likely to work successfully. Do not hesitate to get help from experts in this field and those with local knowledge of the stakeholders. Some organizations have communications specialists, HR functions can often help and BCMs will have good local knowledge.

6.3.2 Stakeholder engagement strategy

> *'We cling to our own point of view, as though everything depended on it. Yet our opinions have no permanence; like autumn and winter, they gradually pass away.'* Chuang Tzu

Chapter 2 sets out the main elements of a governance strategy. As with the other chapters, we will just focus on the specifics here.

Communications only work if all parts of the cycle function correctly:

- Messages must be understandable by the target audience and portray the desired intent.
- The target audience must receive and understand the message.
- The communications must have the desired reaction from the audience.

You will not do all of the engagement. But if you fail to put the basics in place, do not ensure the plan is followed, and do not capture feedback to check if communications are working, you are likely to get the blame if it all goes wrong.

Hints and tips

Never underestimate silent stakeholders: are they supportive, or just waiting for the moment to voice their concerns, or worse?

So here are the specifics that you need to build into your strategy:

- How will stakeholders be identified and evaluated?
- What mechanisms will you use to profile them: for example, how will you measure their support?
- What role will corporate communications have in the programme? What authority do they have on information release?
- How will the internal teams be informed so they have clear messages?
- What communications will be used and by whom?
- Who has the authority to produce communications?
- How will the status and attitude of stakeholders be tracked?
- How will key gatekeepers to each stakeholder group be identified and managed?
- What information sources will be used to maintain stakeholder intelligence?
- How will feedback and reaction be measured?
- How will the communications be funded?

6.3.3 Stakeholder profiling

The first step is to find out who are the stakeholders and start to build a picture of what it is they are interested in. Before going on a stakeholder hunt, it is worth considering other programmes and projects that are running in your organization, as not only are they potentially stakeholders, they may already have done some of this work and be targeting similar groups of stakeholders.

Hints and tips

Do not be mistaken into thinking that you only have to worry about stakeholders who are supportive – they are the least dangerous.

You are looking for people who should have their finger on the pulse of what is going on in the world outside of the programme and who have the contacts in the parts of the organization that the programme will change. They should be able to poll opinions and work out how the audience will need to be engaged with and managed.

To undertake the analysis you need to work out the overall impact that the stakeholders are going to have. Some of the stakeholders will need to play an important active role in the programme. You need to make sure engagement with these encourages them to do so.

So the maintenance of the stakeholder profiles should be an ongoing activity and the engagement status reviewed by the programme board as a standing agenda item.

For each group you should decide what the communications plan needs to achieve, so you will need to work out:

- What level of support you will need from them
- How active they will need to be
- Where are they on the level of engagement at the moment
- What channels are going to work best for them
- Who will be most effective in delivering the message
- When will be the best time to engage them.

An example of the process for identifying and analysing stakeholders is provided in Figure 6.1.

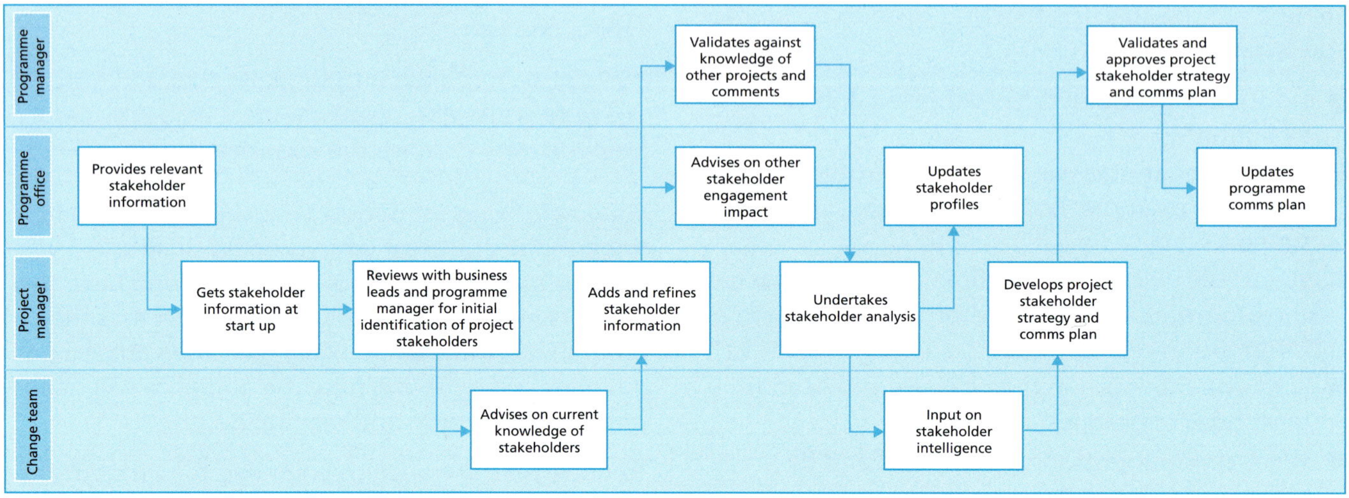

Figure 6.1 Example of the process for stakeholder identification and analysis

6.3.4 Communications plan and delivery

There is always a temptation to run headlong into launches and announcements without fully understanding the audience: equally, delaying communications just raises suspicions that whatever the change is that is coming, it is going to be bad.

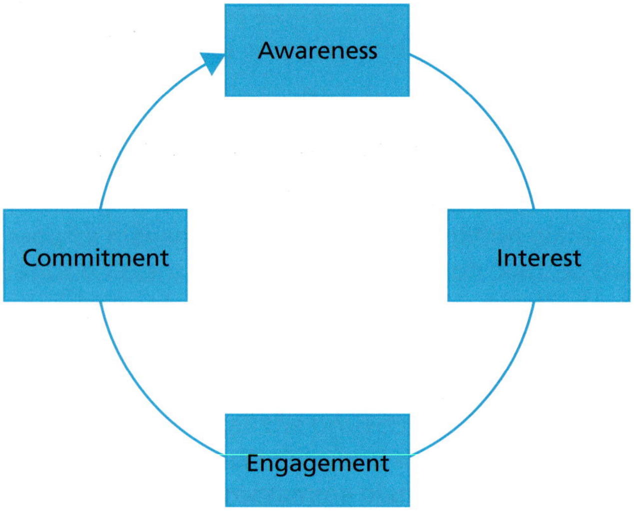

Figure 6.2 Information delivery cycle

It is important when delivering information to take people on a 'journey' and feed them relevant information at the appropriate time. This journey can also be seen as a cycle (see Figure 6.2), which has its origins in sales and marketing.

As an example of such a cycle, a car manufacturer would use general TV advertising to generate awareness of the brand and the features.

6.3.5 Communications procedures

This is a simple process for creating and releasing a message and measuring the effect:

- Identify the event the message is related to, e.g. transition is approaching.
- Understand which stakeholders have an interest, especially those with concerns or objections.
- Determine for each group what you want them to understand and what reaction you want.
- Design the message and method of delivery for each stakeholder/group.
- Design the method to capture feedback.

- Review with a sample of stakeholders, communications/PR experts, especially if the message is critical.
- Engage and communicate.
- Refine outstanding engagements if feedback so requires.

Hints and tips

You don't need to do all of this but you must ensure that it is done by competent, well-briefed people.

6.4 YOUR ROLE IN LEADERSHIP AND STAKEHOLDER ENGAGEMENT

This theme is critical to the programme manager. If communications are handled well then life is likely to be easier for everyone involved in the programme. If it is handled badly then the tough jobs will become exponentially more difficult.

You will need to ensure that the right controls are in place and that there is a stakeholder engagement strategy in place that you have signed up to and the SRO has signed off. The danger is that projects communicate separately from the programme. Apart from showing a lack of control this is also dangerous because the project perspective on a scenario or progress may be different from that of the programme and the wider organization. A particular project could be going very well and be broadcasting positive messages during a period of high stakeholder resistance or the opposite may be happening: negative messages when there is a very positive feel around the programme. So you need to agree how the management controls work and make sure you are in the approval chain.

If your organization has professional communicators use them: their expertise will ensure message clarity.

6.4.1 Business change managers

You will need to get BCMs to work as a team on this, and you may choose to recommend that they include a dedicated communications person in the business change team. It is not a trivial job to do the stakeholder analysis and communications tracking. You definitely do not want to find yourselves in a position where there are conflicting messages coming out of the programme. A good place to start is to ensure that the BCMs are all on the same page when it comes to communications.

6.4.2 Senior responsible owner

With the SRO you will need to work closely. They are likely to be more influential and have better contacts with the executive and powerful influencers and be able to open doors that you cannot. They will also be extremely concerned about maintaining stakeholder engagement and support. They will not want the big players drifting away from the table as their reputation is at stake.

Table 6.1 is a summary of the roles from MSP.

Table 6.1 Areas of focus for the key roles in leadership and stakeholder engagement

Role	Area of focus
Senior responsible owner (SRO)	Engaging key stakeholders early and at appropriate milestones throughout the programme Leading the engagement with high-impact stakeholders and anticipating stakeholder issues that may arise

Role	Area of focus
Senior responsible owner *continued*	Briefing the sponsoring group and gathering strategic guidance on changing business drivers Showing visible leadership at key communications events and ensuring the visible and demonstrable commitment of the sponsoring group Ensuring the creation, implementation and maintenance of the overall stakeholder engagement strategy
Programme manager	Developing and implementing the stakeholder engagement strategy Day-to-day implementation of the whole stakeholder engagement process Developing and maintaining the stakeholder profiles Controlling and aligning project communications activities Ensuring effective communications with the project teams Developing, implementing and updating the programme communications plan
Business change manager(s)	Engaging and leading those operating new working practices through the transition, generating confidence and buy-in from those involved. Active stakeholder engagement is a major part of discharging this role Supporting the SRO and taking specific responsibility for stakeholder engagement in their part of the organization Support to the programme manager in the development of the stakeholder engagement strategy and programme communications plan Alerting the programme manager to the net winners and losers (if any) in their area of change Providing information and business intelligence for the stakeholder profiles Briefing and liaising with the business change team Communicating with affected stakeholders to identify new benefits and improved ways of realizing benefits Delivering key communications messages to their business operations
Programme office	Maintaining information relating to the stakeholders Maintaining an audit trail of communication activity Collating feedback and ensuring that it is logged and processed Facilitating activities specified in the programme communications plan

7

Risk and issue management

7 Risk and issue management

> *'What we anticipate seldom occurs, what we least expect generally happens.'*
> Benjamin Disraeli

Programme managers are responsible for effective risk management in the whole programme. They are not responsible for all risks. For example business change managers (BCMs) are responsible for a couple of the biggest risks, which are that the programme will cause a loss of business performance stability during the change or fail to deliver the benefits on which the investment was justified. Both of these have your name against them so this is a topic you should be very focused on. You must make sure risks have appropriate owners who will ensure they are actively managed.

Some people are very risk-averse, others are too cavalier and some are ostriches burying their heads in the sand and ignoring the risk. The very nature of transformation programmes is that you have to take some risks. At the outset you do not know what will work. You will need to try different solutions to find the optimum approach. Your job is to get the right balance between enough risk so a wide enough range of change options are explored, and avoiding too much risk that can easily lead to disaster.

7.1 BASIC PRINCIPLES

In summary, risks are things that might happen, while issues are things that have happened. Both require management. Supporting them are change control and configuration management, which is often linked to issue management.

Risk management is the management of uncertainty. It can be positive or negative. Most programmes happily occupy themselves with the negative effects but by including the opportunities as well it helps to keep the discussion more positive. In reality successful programmes often do have a bit of luck and with good risk management getting lucky can become a habit. The golfer Gary Player said: 'The more I practise, the luckier I get.'

Risk is real and it has been said that one of the worst things that happened to risk management was the risk register. It gives the impression of risks being linear when, in fact, risks are relational and interconnected. When things go wrong it is the interconnectivity of the risks that causes the major problems; it is rarely a single risk.

This is why it is much better to focus on the threat or the root cause. If you think about the London 2012 Olympics, there was a major threat of a terrorist attack. However, there were many ways it could have occurred and there were many potential effects; breaking down a risk into its component parts can help everyone understand the risk and make it more tangible to manage.

You will probably find that you have a mix of threats, events and effects on your risk register. By focusing on the threats, you can also very quickly reduce the risk register from an endless list of the things that might go wrong to a more focused document where you manage the threats or events rather than worrying about the effects (see Figure 7.1).

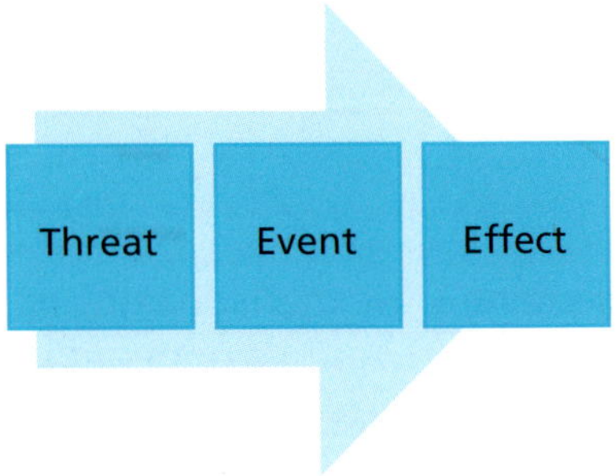

Figure 7.1 Threat, event and effect flow

Issue management is the activity that fills a lot of time for programme teams. If the team is not great at risk management, they end up with too many issues with the danger that the list just keeps growing. You must ensure that there is a way of resolving the issues and also categorizing them in terms of priority and impact.

Change control is the key to effective delivery of the blueprint. It must happen at the programme level but there are dangers at the project level. Individual projects may be working within their permitted tolerances but the aggregating effect of a dozen projects all being 10% over on their budgets or time can have a massive effect on the ability to deliver change and release benefits.

Configuration management is basically version control of assets. Whether the asset is a manufacturing unit, a bill for parliament, IT software or a programme document, it is important that the right one is being used, that it has been authorized and has some sort of version number. This is covered by the information management strategy and is very much in the remit of the programme manager and the programme office.

Hints and tips

The number one cause of programme failure is risks materializing. Some you cannot avoid, but not identifying and trying to treat them is a programme management 'crime'.

7.2 WHAT DOES MSP HAVE TO SAY?

MSP defines a risk as an uncertain event or set of events which, should it occur, will have an effect on the achievement of objectives. This effect need not be detrimental. A risk can be either a 'threat' (i.e. an uncertain event that could have a negative impact on objectives or benefits) or an 'opportunity' (i.e. an uncertain event that could have a favourable impact on objectives or benefits).

Issues are events that have happened, were not planned, are currently affecting the programme in some way and need to be actively dealt with and resolved.

The task of programme risk management is to ensure that the programme makes cost-effective use of a risk management process that includes a series of well-defined steps. The aim is to support better decision-making through a good understanding of risks and their likely impact.

Risks and issues can emerge from a variety of sources – for example:

- Benefits management, transition activities, costs, scope and timescales
- Dependencies, constraints, assumptions, quality of operations, resources and programme deliverables
- Anything that cannot be resolved within a project, or issues common to more than one project

- Stakeholders, organization and programme staff, and third parties
- Degradation of operational performance beyond acceptable levels
- Ambiguity or lack of knowledge about the 'as-is' state, the interim state and the desired end state
- Other projects and programmes under way within the organization.

Effective organizational risk management looks at risk across four perspectives – strategic, programme, operational and project – and as programme manager you must ensure that risks in your programme are managed at the appropriate perspective (see Table 7.1 for risk management perspectives). This means that risks will sometimes need to be escalated or delegated to the appropriate level, and the risk management strategy which you author will give guidance on the escalation process and criteria.

7.2.1 Principles of risk management

The principles of effective risk management for any organization, and hence for its programmes, are that it:

- Aligns with objectives
- Fits the context
- Engages stakeholders
- Provides clear guidance
- Informs decision-making
- Facilitates continual improvement
- Creates a supportive culture
- Increases the likelihood that the programme will achieve measurable value.

Table 7.1 Risk management perspectives

Strategic	Changes at the strategic level can affect the programme, its interdependencies with other initiatives and ultimately its outcomes and benefits realization.
Programme	Programmes focus on delivering benefits to the organization and often affect a wide variety of stakeholders both internally and externally, positively and negatively. Risk management for a programme must be designed to work across organizational boundaries in order to accommodate these differing interests and ensure that stakeholders are engaged appropriately.
Project	The project outputs within a programme are the vehicles for delivering the programme outcomes and benefits; therefore, much of the focus of risk and issue management within a programme is from the project perspective. The programme should set the risk and issue management standards for the project and then give staff the authority to manage their risks and issues within these parameters. To manage the risks to projects well, the programme needs to ensure that each project brief outlines the risks from the perspective of the programme and then request the project to provide regular feedback to the programme's risk management activities.
Operational	As projects deliver their outputs, the transition to new ways of working and new systems can lead to further sources of risk. For example, during a handover process, risks and issues could arise from the need to maintain operational stability as well as the integrity of the systems, infrastructure and support services. Transition must therefore be properly planned, managed and resourced.

7.2.2 Managing risks in a programme

Before the risk management cycle can operate, the specific arrangements for managing risk should specify:

- Risk appetite
- Tolerance thresholds
- Assumptions
- Early-warning indicators
- Risk register content
- Threat and opportunity
- Evaluating risks
- Risk aggregation
- Proximity
- Progress reporting.

There are a number of potential types of response to any risk, namely:

- Avoid a threat or exploit an opportunity
- Reduce a threat or enhance an opportunity
- Transfer the risk
- Share the risk
- Accept the risk
- Prepare contingency plans.

7.2.3 Managing issues in a programme

Issues can occur at any point from the launch of the programme at the beginning of Identifying a Programme to when the programme closes. Some issues may be unresolved at the end of the programme and responsibility for these may need to be transferred to operational management.

An issue is a relevant event that has happened, was not planned and requires management action. The action required may be to fix a problem or to change the boundary of the programme. An issue generally emerges from one of a number of sources, for example:

- Constraints identified at the outset of the programme
- Within the programme itself
- In operational areas to be changed by the programme, where these have a consequential impact on the programme
- Escalated from a programme's constituent projects
- Generated by stakeholders
- Other sources external to the programme (e.g. changes to corporate strategy or conflicts with other concurrent change initiatives).

Issues that occur in a project may need to be escalated if they fall outside the project's tolerance levels set by the programme. Issue management in a programme needs to cover all of these circumstances.

A common cause of overload in a programme is when it tries to manage the project issues directly and does not effectively manage escalation and delegation. However, the programme manager does need to be satisfied that the project teams are managing issues to a satisfactory standard and that the aggregated impact on the programme from all issues in all its projects is understood and acceptable.

Issues can typically be classified into one of the following three types:

- A previously identified risk that has now materialized and requires appropriate issue management action
- A request for change to some aspect of the programme, an operation or a project
- A problem affecting all or part of the programme in some way.

7.2.4 Change control

Programmes are inherently about delivering change but they do not work in isolation as changes are happening in the environment they are delivering to all the time. This can result in changing business requirements, reactions to unplanned events or failures, and loss of stakeholder confidence, all of which can affect the ability of the programme to deliver its objectives. There is a particular risk that small changes across a number of projects may conflict and, because of their apparent insignificance, they may pass through unnoticed.

The basic steps of change control are:

- Capture the change and define why it is needed
- Allocate a priority so that the urgency is understood
- Assess the impact across the programme
- Analyse the options and test the potential solutions
- Authorize the resolution that is agreed (which could include no action)
- Implement the change and monitor the effects of the change for deviations from what is anticipated
- Review the effectiveness and update associated documentation.

All changes should undergo an assessment that considers their impact on at least the following:

- Programme plan
- Blueprint
- Benefits
- Projects dossier.

7.2.5 Configuration management

The purpose of configuration management in a programme is to control the development of, and changes to, items that are important to the programme and the organization. These items include programme management documentation as well as the assets, products and services created by the programme. Configuration management covers the programme's dependencies on items outside of its control as well as those within the programme.

There are five basic processes involved in programme-level configuration management.

- Planning
- Identifying
- Controlling
- Status accounting
- Verifying.

7.3 WHAT DOES THIS MEAN TO YOU?

> *'The first principle is that you must not fool yourself, and you are the easiest person to fool.'* Richard P. Feynman, Nobel-Prize-winning physicist

As the programme manager you are setting up the programme engine room; therefore you need to consider the scope and sources of risks, how they will be managed, and when they become an issue what processes will be used to resolve them.

Risks are where the programme is going to go wrong, and if you aren't in control of them your job will be a nightmare.

The relationship between corporate risk and programme risk needs to be understood. In some circumstances the programme will be creating an organizational risk: for example performance stability during change. It can also be dealing with a corporate risk: for example legislative compliance. It may also be having a number of effects on other corporate risks and their status.

You are responsible for a establishing a clear risk management strategy that sets these things out: this is very important. You will need help with this from risk experts, from BCMs for the operational perspective, from specialists, and from the senior responsible owner (SRO) who approves it. There may be programme risks that have no bearing or impact on corporate risks, so having clear definitions, boundaries and escalation techniques to and from corporate risk is crucial.

Hints and tips

The earlier you put a stake in the ground and embed the risk process the sooner your authority will be felt within the programme. You are not a bystander: you are the one with the toughest job and that needs to be understood.

There are two strategies in this chapter: one covers risk management and the other covers issue management. As with all the strategies, Chapter 2 provides an overview of the common content, so in this chapter we are focusing on the specifics.

There is no reason why you should not amalgamate the strategies, but it is worth remembering that their content is very different.

7.3.1 Risk management

'Risks must be taken because the greatest hazard in life is to risk nothing.' Leo Buscaglia, physicist

When setting out the risk management strategy the following factors should be clearly defined:

- Responsibilities for different types of risks and any specialists that are supporting risk management in the programme
- Interfaces with the corporate risk processes: these are often forgotten and difficult to resolve once the programme is rolling
- Scoring and rating mechanisms: they can be numeric (1 to 5) or alpha (low to high) but there should be a clear description for each level, otherwise the scorings will become random and opinionated
- Processes for capturing and managing strategic and operational risks may be different, as they are not within the programme control
- Escalation routes and triggers for project risks to come to the programme board
- A set of common threats that each project should manage as a risk: this will enable consistent vocabulary, which will in turn enable aggregation – for example resource availability
- Techniques that should be used to calculate risk: for example Monte Carlo simulation, and when it would be used
- How risks will be transferred between programmes or jointly managed – mitigation plans could overlap and nullify each other
- Standards for evaluating and setting risk contingency budgets
- Review and assurance arrangements to check quality of risk management within the projects and also the programme itself.

7.3.1.1 Things to consider

'All courses of action are risky, so prudence is not in avoiding danger (it's impossible), but calculating risk and acting decisively. Make mistakes of ambition and not mistakes of sloth.

Develop the strength to do bold things, not the strength to suffer.' Niccolò Machiavelli

Corporate risk processes which pick up operational risks have a tendency to operate in parallel universe to the programme and project risks. Everyone nods sagely and says this isn't a problem but the fact is that it is a problem. The BCMs are the bridgehead between operations and the programme so you need to encourage them to keep an eye on both universes to ensure that they are aligned and no gaps are developing.

You oversee the projects. You will not manage all the detail of risk in the projects but you must make sure each project is effectively managing risk. The business change team are also going to be working with the projects, so they are your intelligence network, and by having internal discussions you may find you can aggregate issues and risks across the projects and gain a more insightful understanding.

Talk to others who have been involved in transformational change in your organization. What risks did they face? Pay particular attention to risks related to people barriers. Is the organization culture in some areas not conducive to change?

You will need to establish meaningful risk reporting, such as the process outlined in Figure 7.2. You cannot examine every risk in detail – there are not enough hours in the day. But you do need to have a method of testing that risk reporting is accurate. Contemplate formal and informal approaches.

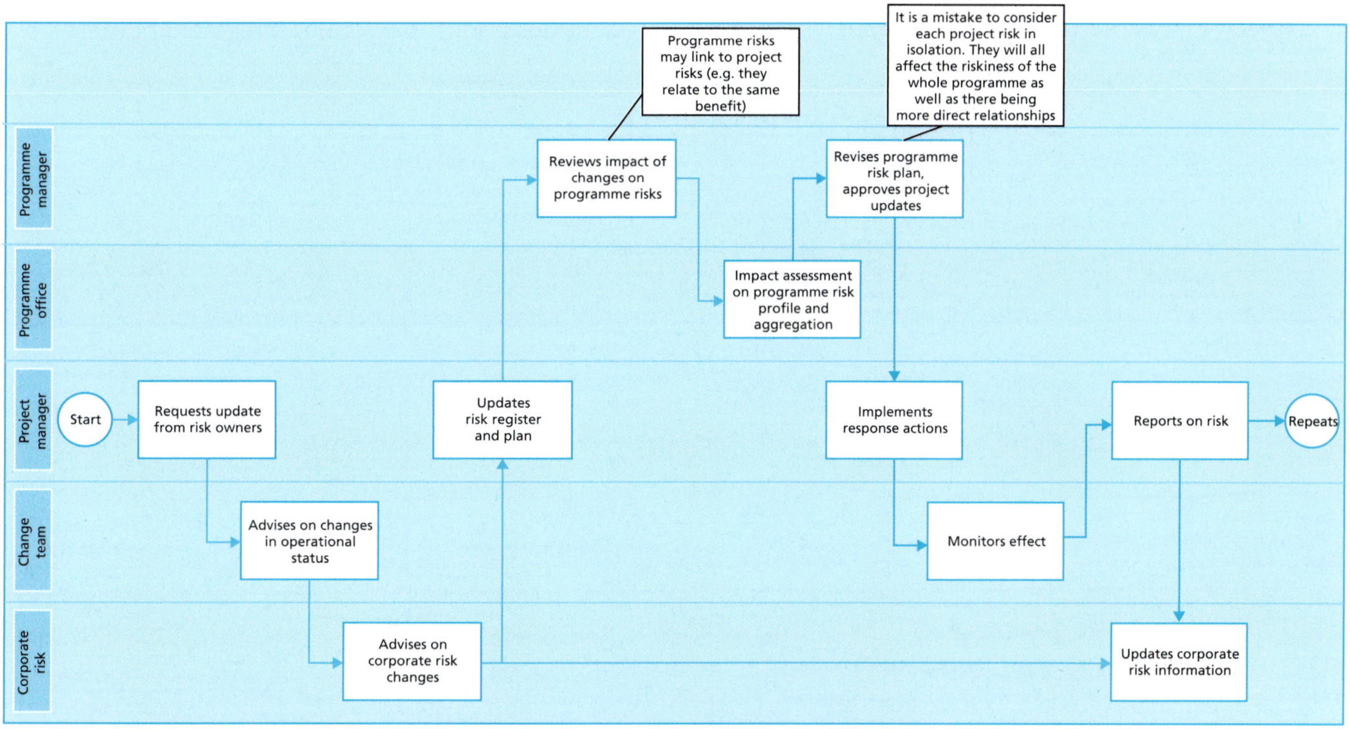

Figure 7.2 Risk management process (project to programme interface)

7.3.2 Issue management

Within MSP, issue management has a wide scope and tends to be what dominates programme activity day to day (see Figure 7.3 for a summary of the process). It is critical that your process has a way of removing issues as well as capturing them, otherwise the issue register just gets bigger and bigger – it sounds obvious but this is easy to overlook.

The specific things that relate to issue management that need to be covered in the strategy should be:

- Weighting scale to enable the severity of the issue to be understood
- Approach to categorization for easier dissemination of issue
- Interfaces with the project issues to enable escalation and definitions of the triggers
- Change control procedures to enable evaluation of the impact of a change and ensure they include benefits and blueprint impact
- Configuration management procedures for storing and tracking assets
- Known or common issues that the projects or business operations will need to manage the impact of
- Interfaces to other groups who may need to be involved with the resolution of issues, in particular, handing over ownership of the issue and tracking it
- Tools to be used, this could be a database or similar and any associated guidance
- Methods for managing change requests to live assets, for example, software or infrastructure
- Responsibilities for checking the effectiveness of changes and closing issues with stakeholders.

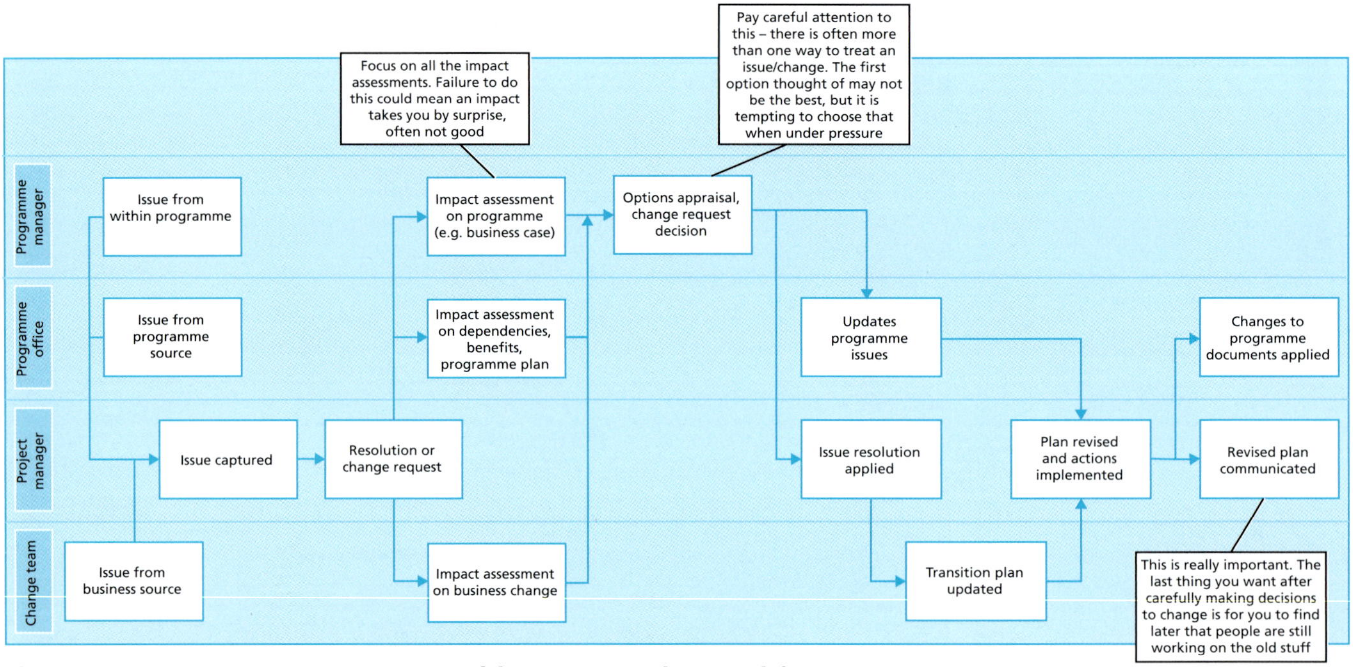

Figure 7.3 Issue management process (change control example)

7.3.3 Risk and issue management cycles

Risk and issue management has the same cycle as you have seen in the other themes (see Figure 2.1). Here are some ideas to help you through because, whether you like it or not, risk and issue management is very important to you and there are things to watch out for.

7.3.3.1 Identify

The programme may have come into existence to manage a potential risk to market or legal position. In that situation much of the risk will be about failure to meet this challenge and the inevitable consequences that follow.

Make sure you are looking beyond individual project and obvious programme risks. There is a particular aspect that will be covered later called 'aggregation', which is the domino or cocktail effect of risks affecting each other (see section 7.3.3.2). Anything that happens in the project world can potentially threaten your benefits and blueprint. Table 7.2 lists the threats that you can use as a checklist during the Identify step of the cycle.

7.3.3.2 Analyse and profile

There tends to be a focus on completing lines of risk in a register but there is value in profiling the risk (in the same way that you would profile a benefit or a stakeholder) to understand the root cause of the threat and how it would manifest itself.

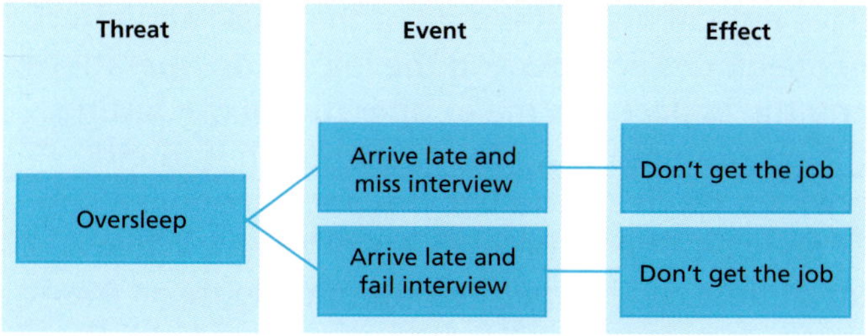

Figure 7.4 Threat, event and effect profile

Example

There was a programme to implement change in an organization's health and safety operation to reduce costs. The consultation with the team started about implementing a different model over the following 18 months. The organization was highly regarded in the market place and there was high demand for experienced and qualified health and safety staff, so rather than wait for redundancy they all started to find new jobs. Within six months the organization was seriously under-resourced and the organization incurred the cost of bringing in freelance consultants.

In the example in Figure 7.4, the threat is the same, but there are a number of ways it could be caused and the effects could be the same or different for each of the events. It is a straightforward illustration, but if you profile risks and build simple maps to show the effects, similar to benefits maps, you will understand the risk much better and the effect it could have on your programme.

Hints and tips

By using a risk map you can illustrate risk in a clearer way than a risk register can.

The result of this profiling work may well make it clear that the programme faces far more risk than was anticipated and may cause the sponsoring group to have a rethink. The earlier this happens the better, as the SRO must accept the level of risk they are taking.

Table 7.2 Threats to look for during the Identify step

Threat	Description
Lack of resource capacity	This may be as a result of inexperience or lack of numbers, but it is almost certain that it will affect the programme, and by ensuring that each project uses this heading to manage its risks you can monitor the aggregating threat.
Inexperienced leadership	It is likely that the leaders will be experienced in leading their operational areas, but they may not have the experience as project or programme leaders in the roles of project sponsors of BCMs; as such the mitigation should be development plans to increase their competence.
Budget changes	Invariably this hits every programme in some way. You need to be particularly wary of small changes across a number of projects that are within their tolerance.
Business performance information	The root cause of many benefits failures is that there is no data to prove they have been achieved. In fact, there is no business performance information at all to prove anything. This will need to be addressed early in the programme as it will also affect the content of the blueprint. One benefit may be the availability of performance data in the future.
Control of business processes	Benefits tend to evaporate because there are uncontrolled changes to ways of working or structures. Consequently when the time comes to harvest a benefit (for example, close a post), the post may have gone two years earlier when someone resigned and it wasn't filled. The same applies to double-counting of benefits: you can only close a post once!
Stakeholder support	This is the root cause of many problems, so you should be monitoring it across the programme. This is a topic in its own right but having it as a standard risk will maintain focus.

When undertaking profiling, consider two areas:

- **Domino or cascade effect** If the threat materializes from one or more events, what other risks could be triggered as well? This could cause a domino effect to occur that would have a bigger impact than the individual risks in isolation.
- **Cocktail effect** If a number of the threats happen simultaneously but are largely unconnected, what would the total effect be? The mitigation plans may be able to cope with one risk materializing but what are the dependencies between plans (e.g. key resources)?

Hints and tips

If you are being burdened by issues, it means that your risk management is not working.

For you to be effective, it is critical to ensure you have a good understanding of the cause and effect between project risks and the impact on operations, and the impact of a major operational risk hitting the programme or a project. Although it sounds obvious, be clear whether you are managing a risk or an issue. The techniques are different. While a lot of time can be spent trying to mitigate an event that is certain to happen (the issue), it may be the effects of the event that are uncertain. It is these that present the risk and must be managed.

Example

If your programme could be affected by an upcoming election, the election is an issue as it is going to happen and you will have to deal with the consequences. The risk is a change of political direction, which could have legislative impact on your programme.

7.3.3.3 Measure and plan

There are two big areas to consider: risks relating to operational readiness and ability to sustain the change, and the capability that the projects are building being available on time and functioning.

Each of the risks should have contingency plans in place to deal with the 'what if' scenarios should situations materialize.

You should produce a probability/impact grid like the one shown in Table 7.3 to help plan the intensity of the management of individual risks; the ones with high probability and high impact are going to receive a lot more focus than those that are perceived to be under control.

The use is related to the escalation of risks to a higher level, and the visual portrayal of the risks of your programme to those stakeholders who need it. If populated with the risks of the programme, this is a tool which helps evaluate the risk exposure of the programme, and is called a summary risk profile.

7.3.3.4 Deliver and review

The effectiveness of the management of risk will be reflected in the size of the issue register: if it is large then it will mean that the risks are not being well managed, but that is often the reality of the situation. It is particularly a problem with emergent programmes because many of the projects are already rolling and difficult to bring under control, so issues tend to dominate. You should keep a close eye on project risks and issues and how they may trigger problems for you.

The key concern of the programme manager should be the effective management of programme-level risks, ensuring they are assigned appropriate owners and brought within tolerance, assessing and communicating the aggregated level of risk to the programme, and the relationship between the risks and identified issues of the programme. Risk aggregation is important here. For example, when

Table 7.3 Example of a probability/impact grid

Shading indicates priority of risk: dark = high; medium = average; light = low

Impact/likelihood	Very low	Low	Medium	High	Very high
Highly likely					
Likely					
Medium					
Unlikely					
Highly unlikely					

you are looking at project risk you are trying to determine those that have a broader impact than just the project and may therefore require attention at the programme level.

Quite often the level of danger is hidden within pages and pages of a risk register. It may be useful to draw the potential relationship between risks, as illustrated in Figure 7.5. This captures your risks on a 'radar' so that you can see how they are interrelated and if they are moving around.

In the simple example shown in Figure 7.5, risk A could trigger risk E and so could risk B. If risks E and B are becoming more likely, the overall level of risk will be rising, as will the potential impact.

In real life, a chart such as that shown in Figure 7.5 often ends up needing an A3 sheet to show all the risks, but it is much more effective in getting the attention of people than wading through pages of paper at each project board. If nothing else, produce something like this for the risks that affect you and use it to communicate with your teams.

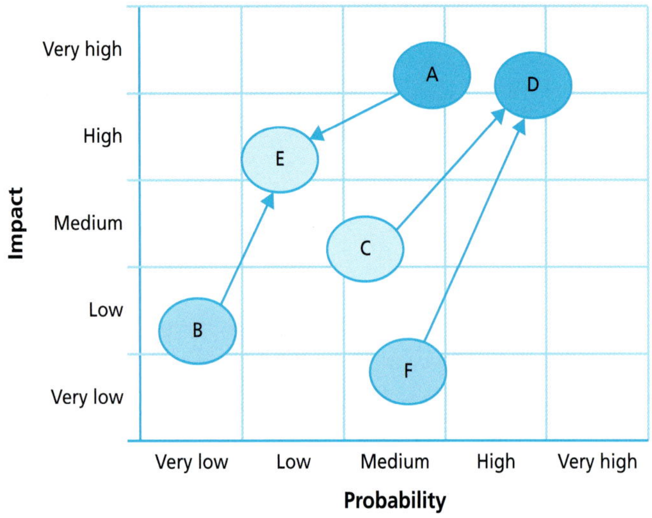

Figure 7.5 Tracking aggregated risks

> **Example**
>
> A project has a risk that one of its suppliers might go out of business. That is not critical for that project so it has not escalated the risk. However the programme is aware that several future projects not yet started will depend on the same supplier in a more critical way. The programme may need to take action now.

7.4 YOUR ROLE IN RISK AND ISSUE MANAGEMENT

The roles and areas of focus table (Table 7.4) is taken from MSP and sets out the specific areas of focus that MSP has defined for you and the other roles; as you can see most of the responsibility sits with the programme manager.

The processes and tools that are used will be your responsibility, so you need to work closely with others who will use them to ensure they work for them and are pragmatic. You should make sure that they also have their finger on the pulse of the project and programme risks. The big areas you must know about are anything that threatens the blueprint or the benefits.

7.4.1 Business change managers

As always BCMs need to build a relationship and work as a team. It is likely that the risks will be similar for all of them, but the local effects will be different. The aggregating effect of risks across the organization will be one of the key areas for BCMs to work on.

7.4.2 Senior responsible owner

For the SRO risks are the things that are going to cost them their job if they miss something important. It isn't unknown for SROs to want to bury their heads in the sand about the reality of the situation and take the position 'just sort it out', which creates a particularly dangerous culture of risk suppression. Their focus will be on the strategic risks so bear that in mind. In your relationship with the SRO you will need to find a way to engage them constructively and provide honest and open advice. Try to not to be the bearer of problems; try to bring forward the problem and some potential solutions to help them with the decision.

7.4.3 Project teams

Project teams will manage their own risks (including those on the standard checklist), unless they need to escalate them. Make sure it is clear to projects when and how this will happen. Some risks identified in the programme will be delegated to projects. Make sure they know what to do with them. You will need to aggregate risk. To do this you must make sure the processes and standards that projects use are consistent across the entire programme. Otherwise aggregation will fail or produce meaningless results.

Table 7.4 Areas of focus for the key roles in risk and issue management

Role	Area of focus
Senior responsible owner (SRO)	Authorizes the risk management strategy and issue management strategy and its adjustment, improvement and enforcement
	Intervenes to control risks and issues that affect the alignment of the programme with organizational objectives
	Initiates assurance reviews of risk and issue management effectiveness
	Has ownership of strategic risks and issues, and ensures mitigation actions are dealt with at the appropriate senior level
Programme manager	Develops and implements the strategies for handling risks and issues
	Designs and manages the risk and issue management cycle
	Manages the aggregated level of risks and issues
	Assures programme adherence to the risk management principles
	Allocates risks and issues as appropriate
	Ensures that change control is undertaken by individuals with the correct authority
	Ensures that the impact of individual and aggregated risks is understood by the relevant stakeholders
	Defines clear rules for escalation, cascade and thresholds
	Has ownership of programme-level risks and issues
	Deploys a consistent language for risk management across the programme and its projects
	Communicates progress on the resolution of issues in a clear and timely fashion across the programme
	Escalates items that cross programme boundaries to the SRO for resolution where necessary
	Design and implementation of the configuration management system

Role	Area of focus
Business change manager(s)	Manages and coordinates the resolution of risks relating to operational performance and benefits achievement Ensures that the risk management cycle includes operational risks Manages risks that impact on business performance and transition Identifies operational issues and ensures that they are managed by the programme Identifies opportunities from the business operations and raises them for inclusion in the programme Contributes to impact assessments and change control Monitors and reports on business performance issues that may require the attention of the programme during transition
Programme office	Manages and coordinates the information and support systems to enable efficient handling of the programme's risks and issues Maintains the programme risk register Maintains the programme issue register Establishes, facilitates and maintains the risk management cycle Establishes, facilitates and maintains the issue management cycle Provides support and advice on the risks and issues to projects Coordinates risk and issue management interfaces with projects Maintains the configuration management system Facilitates the change control steps

8 Planning and control

8 Planning and control

> *'Those who plan do better than those who do not plan even though they rarely stick to their plan.'* Winston Churchill

This theme isn't called planning and control by accident. It is in two parts: the first covers developing the programme plan and the second covers controlling the programme delivery based on the plan.

From your point of view as the programme manager, a lot of the detail concerning planning revolves around capability building and project delivery, because this is where the money is going to be spent, and everyone worries about money.

Part of the reason why benefits tend to be forgotten about is because all the focus goes on building things rather than what happens once they are built and how the benefits will be released.

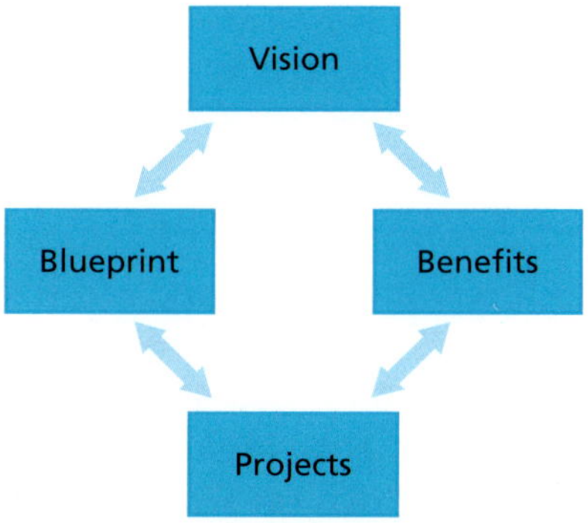

Figure 8.1 The relationship between vision, blueprint, benefits and projects

Planning brings together the vision, the blueprint and benefits and helps to define the projects needed to enable the requirements for them to be met (see Figure 8.1). So, if you have projects and no benefits or blueprint, something is going to go wrong. An example of the planning process is illustrated in Figure 8.2.

Example

An English city council was undertaking a major transformation that would restructure and change the ways of working for almost the entire organization. A structure of projects, programmes and a portfolio was put in place. Reporting was established early on, with projects reporting to programmes then to the portfolio board. People working in the portfolio would declare with pride that they were in control. About nine months into the work an independent review was conducted. There were very few up-to-date plans, and a significant number of projects and programmes had no plans at all! Plans were produced to a common approach, and while this revealed that there was a lot of work to be done that had not previously been identified at least they now had basic control.

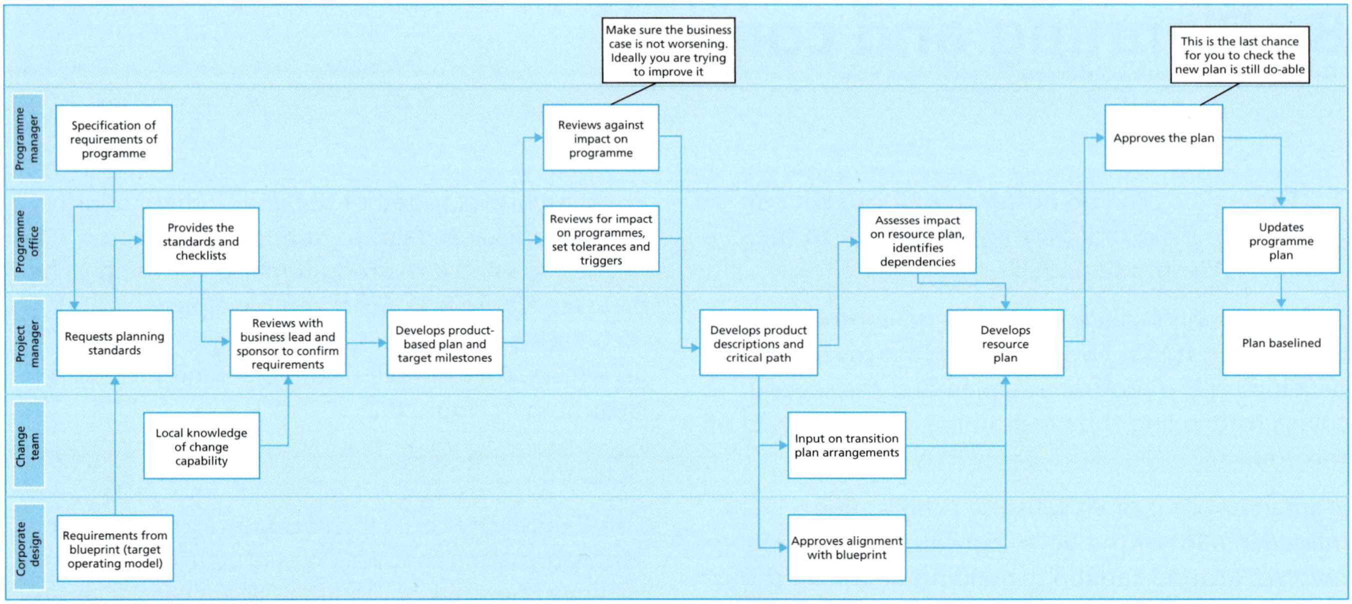

Figure 8.2 Example of the planning process (plan development)

8.1 BASIC PRINCIPLES

'Plans are nothing; planning is everything.'
Dwight D. Eisenhower

This section provides a brief summary of the key concepts within the planning and control theme.

The **programme plan** is often an amalgam of other documents. Within MSP there are a number of plans that need to be developed and managed; for example, the quality and assurance plan, resource management plan, risk mitigation plans, transition plans and benefits realization plan. So the programme plan could be one document with many parts or comprise a number of separate documents.

What the programme plan isn't is a massive chart which shows what all the projects are doing. That is the programme schedule, and if that is what you are seeing as the programme plan, then it is quite probably already out of control.

Projects dossier is the MSP term used for the collection of projects that the programme will deliver to create the capability. It is rather an odd phrase and some organizations use the term project portfolio instead, but this can be confused with portfolio management. Increasingly, the term project register is being used for the document that contains all the project information. It should contain enough information to initiate a project and the contents will evolve as the programme progresses; more or fewer projects may be required depending on how things pan out.

Tranches are a very important and often missing concept underpinning control. Programmes often become unwieldy due to their size and tranches help to manage that. They are used to group projects and focus efforts on achieving a 'step change' in capability; this avoids lots of expenditure on many fronts with no clarity about how it all comes together. Tranches are time- and achievement-bound. They are closely linked to the blueprint intermediate states; at the end of a tranche an intermediate state will have been delivered.

Tranches provide an opportunity to stand back, take stock and decide whether the blueprint end state is still where you want to go; whether the benefits are validated, genuine and achievable; and whether you can still afford to get there. It is also an opportunity either to gracefully exit the programme if it is no longer required or to re-energize it if it has lost some momentum.

Workstreams are a way of grouping projects by types so that resources can be concentrated and dedicated to certain activities; for example, you could have a property workstream or an ICT workstream. These are not bound by time and a workstream could run through the life of the programme. Workstreams are put in place as another lens through which to view and control the programme and its tranches.

A **dependency network** is a technique that helps to illustrate how the various elements of the programme fit together, rather like a jigsaw puzzle. It is a key element of control as it shows how the inputs and outputs from the various projects fit together. It provides the basis for the programme plan critical path, as where a project is dependent on another project, any delays will have knock-on consequences.

Transition plans are the responsibility of the business change managers (BCMs). However, you are likely to have more planning experience than most BCMs and therefore your guidance on how to produce the transition plan could be important. They are inherently linked to the benefits realization plan. The transition plans cover taking the capability, putting it into live operation and turning it into the outcomes. The plan is essential to enable business performance control. Ad hoc changes mean that you lose control and it will be harder to maintain control of the 'as-is' state. The Realizing the Benefits process in the transformational flow provides a lot of pointers to help you with this.

> **Example**
>
> An English city council was undertaking a major transformation that would restructure and change the ways of working for almost the entire organization. In the portfolio only rudimentary thought had been given to dependencies.
> As plans were prepared in ignorance of real dependencies they were not realistic, but the programme teams didn't understand why. Each programme and project was asked a number of questions such as 'Where will the refurbished offices some from?', 'Who will provide the new IT systems?', 'Will your revised services need some of the new shared services to be in place?' etc. As these questions were answered it became clearer how cross-programme and project dependencies would affect timescales, and how setting aside time for collaboration was critical.

8.2 WHAT DOES MSP HAVE TO SAY?

Planning and control are key to the success of any transformation programme and should be seen as distinctly separate concepts and activities.

8.2.1 Programme planning

The preparation of the programme plan involves:

- Processing large amounts of information
- Extensive consultation
- Building the plan.

During its early iterations the programme plan will include many unknowns and a high level of ambiguity. Developing the plan should include:

- Resources
- Resource management strategy and plans
- Risk management
- Projects dossier
- Deadlines and constraints
- Scheduling
- Priorities.

See Figure 8.3 for those elements that impact on the programme plan.

8.2.2 Programme control

Programme control provides supporting activities and processes that run throughout the lifecycle of the programme to:

- Refine and improve delivery
- Minimize the impact of ambiguity
- Bring certainty wherever possible
- Justify the continuance of the programme.

The management and control of the programme should be based on experiences from the previous tranches. Programme control should consider and develop:

- Monitoring and control strategy
- Dependency management
- Starting projects
- Integration of information
- Progress monitoring
- Project control
- Planning and controlling transition.

8.2.3 Transition management

While an estimate of the length of the transition period should be considered when developing the overall programme plan, more detailed transition planning is not practical until sufficient progress

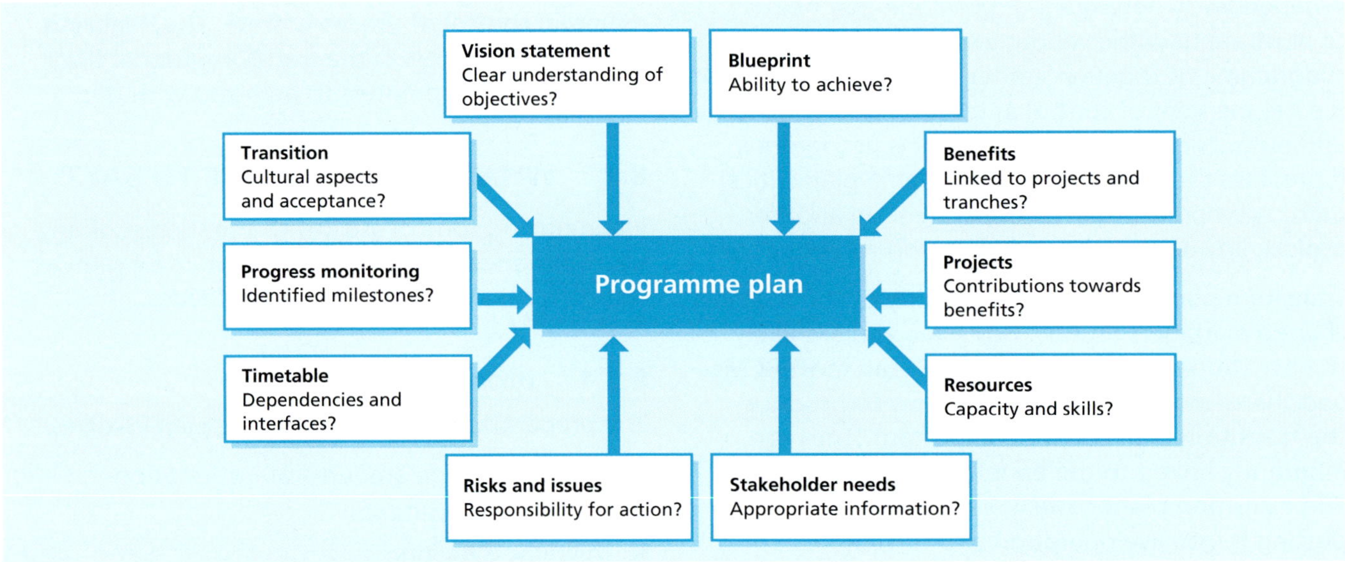

Figure 8.3 Contributions to the programme plan

has been made in each individual tranche. Detailed transition planning requires both knowledge of the specific project outputs and the state of readiness of the operations which are due to change.

MSP defines three phases of transition that should be planned for:

- Pre-transition
- Transition
- Post-transition.

8.3 WHAT DOES THIS MEAN TO YOU?

> *'No matter how good you are at planning, the pressure never goes away. So I don't fight it. I feed off it. I turn pressure into motivation to do my best.'* Benjamin Carson

You are responsible for most of the plans and when preparing them you need to be conscious of the tendency towards optimism. It is a phenomenon that has come through strongly from P3M3 maturity assessments; organizations generally have very few standards when it comes to creating plans and they tend to be a long list of estimates that are all optimistic. It is not that they can't estimate how long it will take to do specific design and build tasks, the problem is more often allowing enough time for other activities. For example risk contingency is often overlooked, so when things go wrong there is not enough slack to absorb the extra work. The aggregating effect is that there is a tremendous sense of optimism and later failure comes as a surprise; this happens repeatedly, which is the real surprise.

It is therefore a good strategy on your part to plan like a pessimist to help balance the approach.

8.4 SETTING UP THE STRATEGIES

Within MSP there are two strategies: the monitoring and control strategy which focuses on how to ensure the programme operates optimally, and the resource management strategy which focuses on where you will find the people and assets to get the programme delivered.

8.4.1 Monitoring and control strategy

As with all strategies, Chapter 2 of this guide provides the main headings. If you are in an organization with a portfolio office, much of this will be pre-defined, but you will still have to work out how to adopt it. Here are some specifics for your monitoring and control strategy:

- The success criteria against which the programme will be managed
- How the reporting processes will work across the programme, projects and business operations
- Standards the projects will be expected to adhere to in the way they operate: for example templates
- Specific techniques that will be used to measure progress: for example earned value for tracking progress
- A common lifecycle and gate control process for projects within the programme – this will provide their basis for planning
- Meeting management arrangements and standards: for example programme boards
- Levels of delegated authority for decision-making
- Terms of reference for any boards or working groups
- Anticipated changes and evolutions to the way governance and controls are applied in different processes and tranches

- What metrics will be used to provide evidence of the success of the management of the programme (e.g. levels of outstanding issues).

The monitoring and control strategy is implemented as part of the programme plan.

8.4.2 Resource management strategy and plan

As with all strategies, Chapter 2 provides the main headings, but here are some specifics for your resource management strategy:

- Assets will be a key resource, not just people, so you must consider what you are going to need
- Accommodation, desk space and supporting infrastructure provision should be included in this strategy
- The balance between internal and external resources, how this will be managed and knowledge from external experts transferred into your organization: this can be a benefit
- Procurement processes that you will use
- How operational assets will be accessed to enable changes to be made: for example parts of a building
- What you will need from your supply chain in terms of people and assets
- Contract management methods that you will use
- Performance management approach to in-house teams
- Supply chain performance regime for provider
- HR standards and policies that will be followed.

The challenge is twofold; to ensure firstly that the strategy covers all the needs for transition and organizational support as well as resourcing the needs of the projects; secondly that the resources required will be available when needed. Some of the resources needed may be allocated to other programmes or projects; or may have priority operational duties.

8.4.3 Dependency management

There is a myth that dependencies are between whole projects and programmes themselves and that is how they can be managed. The unfortunate fact is that the key dependencies are quite often buried deep within each of the projects or business area activities, and the criticality of the dependencies to the overall programme may not be visible to individual project managers.

A dependency network is needed to track the change interactions that create the potential and capability to achieve the intended outcomes.

MSP has always been quite clever in these areas, seeing projects as black boxes which require inputs and outputs. Your role is to take a helicopter view of projects and manage the dependencies. Unfortunately the project management vocabulary doesn't match up to this neat model of inputs and outputs. Hence, projects will use the terms that make it difficult to see the wood for the trees, e.g. product, deliverables (outputs) and assumptions (inputs). You need to address this in your monitoring and control strategy.

Dependencies come in many shapes and forms: apart from being specific project outputs they can include policy statements, decisions, designs, operational changes, external decisions, resources, funding, plans, contracts and procurements in addition to the more obvious deliverables.

8.4.3.1 Nesting dependencies

Many organizations have a number of programmes operating, and in some cases are establishing portfolio management as well; we need to recognize and standardize on our vocabulary. Portfolio management will offer little benefit if it cannot deliver effective dependency management.

Prior to the establishment of the programme there are likely to be dependencies between individual projects (Figure 8.4). Once the programme has been set up, you are likely to encounter three types:

- **Intra-dependencies** These are the dependencies that can be managed within the boundary of a single programme (Figure 8.5). They reflect how the projects depend on each other to deliver the blueprint and the benefits. Projects with dependencies outside the boundary should have these managed by the programme.
- **Interdependencies** These extend beyond the programme boundary and into other programmes (Figure 8.6). They are external to individual programmes but are still within the perimeter of the programme and project management (PPM) environment, and are most likely linked to the scope of the corporate programme management office.
- **Extra-dependencies** These extend beyond the boundaries of all the programmes into other parts of the organization (Figure 8.7). They are outside the control of the PPM community, and are often linked to business as usual (BAU) changes, external dynamics such as legislation, market forces, and strategic decisions and approvals. In an organization with corporate portfolio management, valuable services in the support of managing dependencies can be provided because the portfolio has a broader sphere of influence and control.

In Figures 8.4 to 8.7 the rectangles are outputs, and the circles are inputs.

In reality the dependencies that hold up most programmes are the extra-programme dependencies. They can often be political or economic in nature, and must be tracked through the risk register.

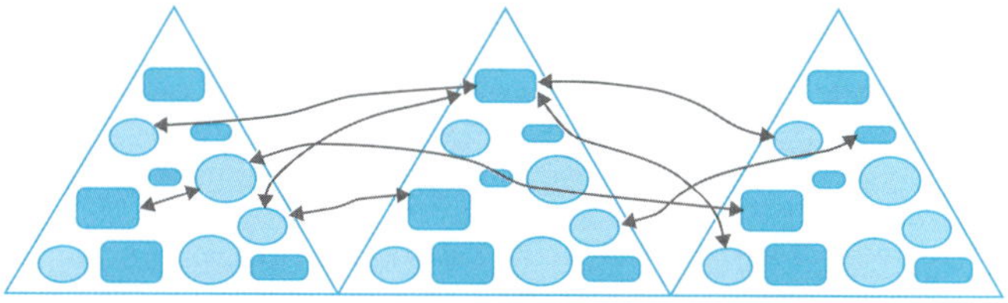

Figure 8.4 Dependencies between individual projects before a programme is established

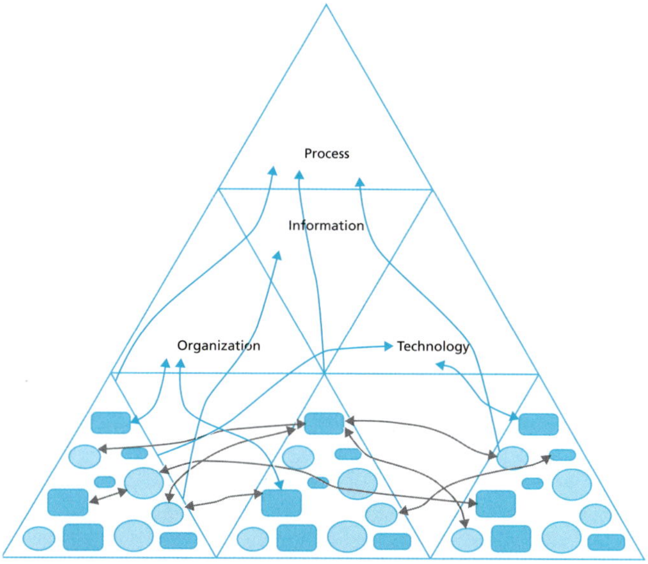

Figure 8.5 Intra-dependencies between individual projects are managed within the programme

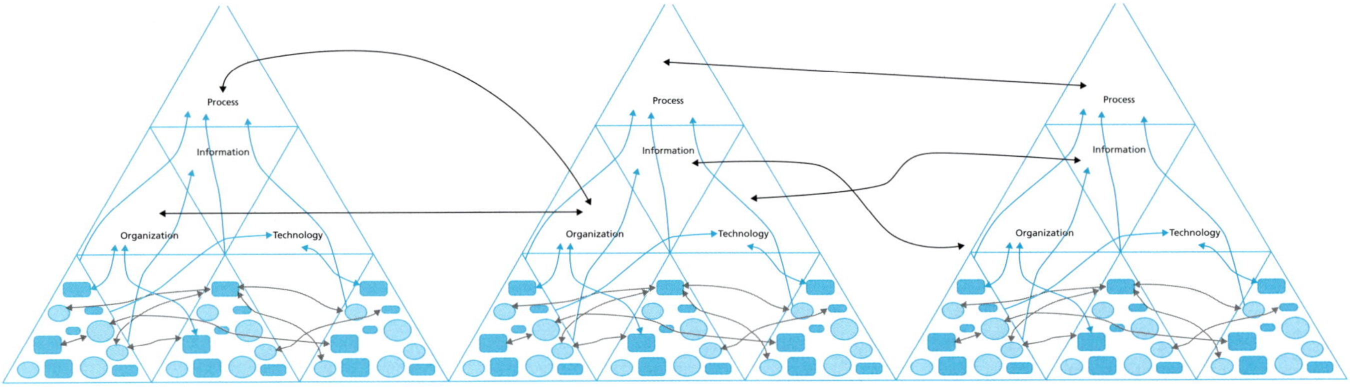

Figure 8.6 Interdependencies are external to individual programmes but are within the PPM environment

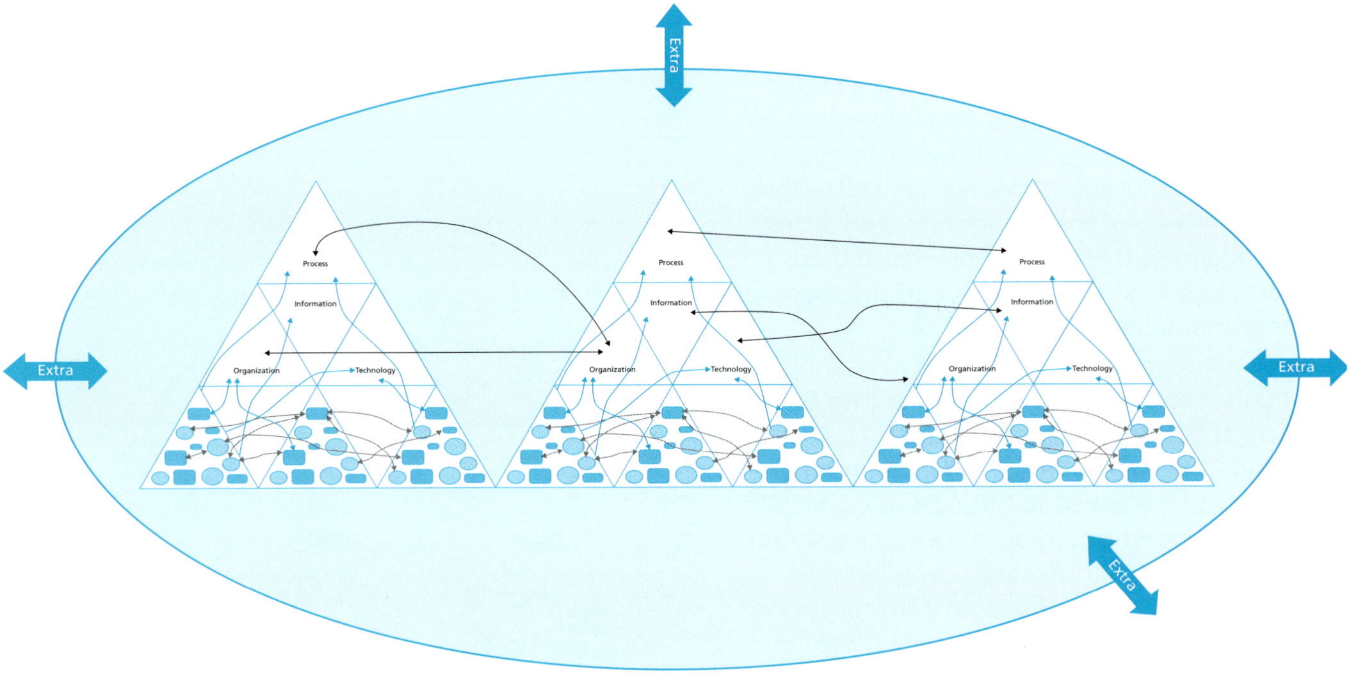

Figure 8.7 Extra-dependencies are outside the control of the PPM community

Our experience has been that the inability to manage dependencies goes back to some very basic standards that are missing, namely planning. To have effective intra-programme dependency management in place there need to be common practices within the projects. PRINCE2 and other project management methods all highlight the value of output-based planning and include it as a core concept, and yet when undertaking reviews we find project managers responding to questions about planning standards with the phrase 'MS Project'. Much of the planning is activity-based rather than product-based and very few have critical paths defined.

Without this underpinning consistency you are trying to compare apples with pears. You can't identify and track project dependencies unless there is a clearly defined product set.

The intra-programme dependencies are well recognized as important, but rarely managed well. As this is your job, don't underestimate it. This is the level you should be operating at, not in the detail of the project plans, unless you find that the dependencies aren't manageable and you need to intervene.

At the inter-programme dependency level the situation deteriorates. The likelihood is that dependency management is happening through informal soft systems, communications and programme managers discussing the dependencies on various projects. At this level it is not possible to track the dependencies down to the project level; we need to have a different currency to express our understanding of the dependencies. We argue strongly that this currency should be the programme blueprints.

The blueprint is the end state that the programme will deliver, and in a multi-programme environment there is always the risk that programmes are planning to change the same areas. A blueprint expresses the organization's future state in terms of processes, people and structures, tools and technology and the management information that will be used to run it.

By overlaying the blueprints to view the overall picture, individual programmes can see how other programmes can contribute to their 'future state' and avoid duplication and gain shared prioritization criteria – and, of course, their interdependencies.

The problem here is that if the other programmes don't have blueprints, dependencies are a random concept equating to managing the wind, i.e. it is impossible. Additionally the blueprints will need to be developed to a consistent standard (defined by the portfolio) to enable the overlaying of blueprints. However, techniques like TOGAF or Output Relationship Modelling can establish a high-level map of dependencies.

If portfolio management is not in place then extra-programme dependencies will need to be owned by individual programme boards to resolve.

8.4.3.2 Things to consider

Here are three things to consider when implementing your dependency network:

- **Establish a standard approach to project planning** This enables you to track the input and output relationship between projects.
- **Review all the current projects and identify their assumptions and deliverables** Build these into a matrix so that you know who is going to be waiting for the deliverable (output) and who is owning the assumption (input). If nobody is

waiting for the deliverable you may ask why resource is being dedicated to its production, and if nobody is owning the assumptions you have an issue that needs to be managed.

- **Ensure that each programme has a blueprint** It is important that organizations have a common standard for developing blueprints, or the problem of planning inconsistencies will move up to the programme level.

Putting it into practice is not so simple; we would recommend you use a matrix to show how the dependencies fit together, as this is a technique we have employed successfully. It should become your management tool for the programme plan. Table 8.1 is an example of such a matrix.

The concept is simple enough: on one axis you have the projects and other sources, while on the other axis you have the name of the product on which you are dependent. From this you can see not only who is creating the product, but who is going to use it, as dependencies are often multiple.

Within project documentation you may find assumptions or things being put out of scope. In a programme someone has to own it otherwise it will not happen – miracles don't tend to happen in programmes!

This provides an at-a-glance view of how everything fits together, and if you add a column to the right of each output, you can add the date when it will be delivered. This will probably highlight gaps and over-optimism. You can then work on lining up the dates between the projects or other sources. Finally you are managing the dependencies.

8.4.4 Building the programme plan

Plans are critical. Without them the programme team will not know where it is going, where it is now and will be out of control. You are responsible for establishing the governance for this in the monitoring and control strategy. Make sure what you put in place is pragmatic: if in doubt err on the simpler side. People often believe that because programmes are complex they must have equally complex and sophisticated planning and reporting tools. Unless these are well established and supported by experienced staff, such tools are likely to make matters worse. Keep it as simple as possible.

Table 8.1 Dependency matrix

	Project A	Project B	Project C	Programme A	Ops area	External org
Business process model	I	I	I		O	
IT software package	O		I		I	
Resource contract	I	I	O			
Accommodation transition plan		O		I	I	I

Key: I = input; O = output.

Note that this table is not a binary calculation. O is where output is created, and I is where it is used.

Hints and tips

If you are qualified in MSP, PRINCE2 and APM or PMI, you will have had roughly 15 days' training, of which less than three will actually be on planning: so recognize your own potential weaknesses sooner rather than later.

Having a coherent and tested capability ready for transition is the prime concern of yourself and the BCMs. What the programme team have committed to in the blueprint needs to be delivered. The projects will be looking after creating the outputs, but you need to oversee this to ensure they are assembled into a properly functioning capability through whatever means are appropriate (see Figure 5.1).

While your focus is more on oversight of the project, preparing the organization for the new operating model is equally as important. This is the area of focus for the BCMs, but the two are not inseparable. The projects must produce good outputs, the programme must assemble them into a tested capability and the operational people must be ready, willing and able to use the capability effectively. You and the BCMs must collaborate, and as transition approaches this will be more hour-by-hour than day-by-day.

The detailed transition plans sit in the operational area. These transition plans need to be aligned with those for the benefits, the projects and the programme, drawing together the various aspects into a format that can be understood by the programme board. As such, some ingenuity in how the plan is presented may well be required.

You can present the programme plan as a series of overlays to aid understanding. Tranches, projects, transition and post-transition are the base plan and provide the 'background' view onto which you place other plans. The dark-tinted boxes show examples of what could be in the benefits realization plan (see Figure 8.8).

In the example provided in Figure 8.8, the 'base' programme plan shows the overall timescale, which projects belong to each tranche, and when change takes place in transition.

The second part of the figure shows how benefits realization activities could be overlaid onto the 'base' plan.

Another overlay could be for quality. Events could be overlaid relative to other activities, the results of which are subject to a quality review. Before a new capability is transitioned into live use it needs to be tested as a complete system. If the capability activities in Figure 8.8 represent the assembly of the system from the separate project outputs then quality reviews can be overlaid next to the capability activities.

The key is about maintaining balance between the effort that is invested in delivering the new capability and the rate of change that the organization can absorb.

Your focus is making sure that the programme plan fits with the drivers and the requirements of the organization. This may result in demand for faster implementation or there may be reasons why the programme needs to slow down. The timescales and priorities will be driven from the programme board and should reflect the drivers and deadlines for change and the ability to absorb it.

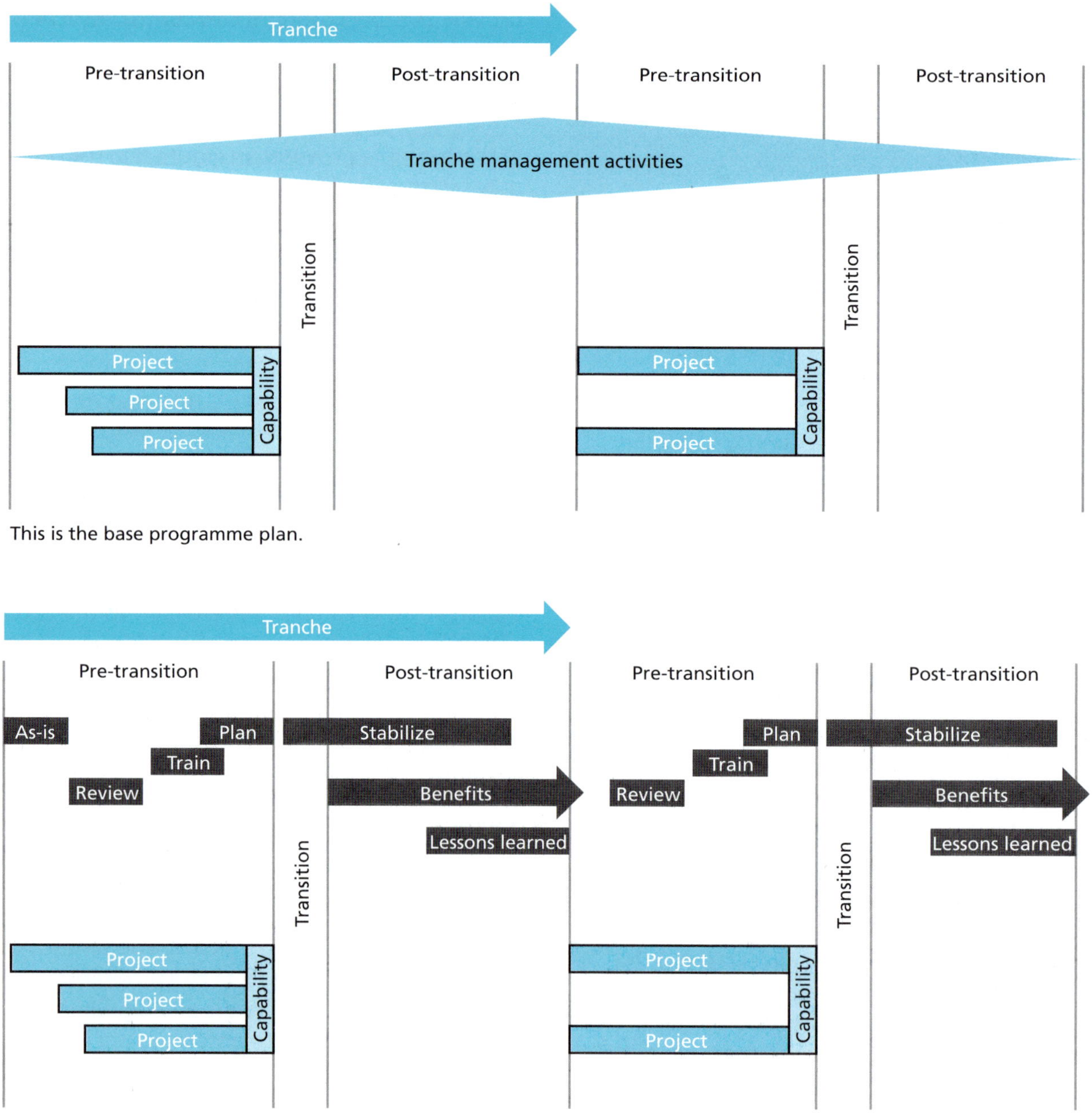

The black tinted boxes show examples of what could be in the benefits realization plan.

Figure 8.8 Base programme plan overlaid with benefits realization activities

8.5 YOUR ROLE IN PLANNING AND CONTROL

'If you can stay calm, while all around you is chaos, then you probably haven't completely understood the seriousness of the situation.' Anonymous

As programme manager you will be under pressure to deliver faster and at a lower cost. However you can't afford to over-compromise on quality as it will affect the benefits. The blueprint is absolutely vital to your role. If you haven't got one then the potential for failure will be much higher. You are responsible for creating the resource management strategy and resourcing much of the programme team. The BCM team should be included as part of developing the resource management plan as they are often best placed to acquire operational resources.

It is tempting to see planning and control as just your domain. To some extent it is but you need to heavily involve others – especially the BCMs. They may well bring technical expertise and experience needed but the BCMs will be bringing the organizational expertise to support them: as with all things in a programme, it is a team effort.

8.5.1 Business change managers

BCMs will always be under pressure to deliver change faster and release the benefits. The big issue is maintaining control; to achieve that, first they must have decent plans to work from. Different parts of an organization will be able to transition at different rates. Some will be more adaptable and flexible while others will be more rigid and resistant, but this will probably reflect the nature of their functions. If you do not consider what other changes an operational unit has been through recently and may go through before your transition, you could find the people suffering from change overload. They are then likely to resist the changes you want to implement. If a portfolio office or similar is established, this might be a good place to go to gain and understanding of what other changes the organization is planning. All this will need to be fed into the transition and benefits realization plans.

8.5.2 Senior responsible owner

With the SRO your relationship will be about ensuring realism about what the projects and organization can achieve within the timescales. The SRO will be driven by timescales that are often beyond their control and are inflexible. They also have their reputation to protect so they will want ambitious timescales but not crazy ones.

8.5.3 Project teams

Project teams will need to develop their plan to dovetail into the overall programme plan. There will be dependencies between projects. You need to make sure they understand this and have access to the programme information they will need. You will need to ensure projects set up monitoring to fit in with the programme's own reporting cycle, and that reports from all projects are produced to consistent standards so they can be consolidated effectively as part of the overall programme reports. Table 8.2 shows the MSP key roles and areas of focus for planning and control.

'You can get a programme manager to commit to an impossible deadline, but you cannot get him to meet it.' Geoff Reiss

Table 8.2 Areas of focus for the key roles in planning and control

Role	Area of focus
Senior responsible owner (SRO)	Consulting with the sponsoring group and other key stakeholders, maintaining their buy-in, especially in preparing for and carrying out transition
	Leading the ongoing monitoring and review activities of the programme, mid-tranche and end-of-tranche, including commissioning formal reviews such as audits/health checks, if required
	Monitoring progress and direction of the programme at a strategic level and initiating management interventions where necessary
	Authorizing the resource management strategy
	Authorizing the monitoring and control strategy
	Ensuring that adequate assurance is designed into the control mechanisms
	Authorizing the projects dossier, programme plan, and the required monitoring and control activities
Programme manager	Designing the projects dossier, resource management strategy, monitoring and control strategy and the required assurance activities
	Designing the programme plan
	Ensuring that the blueprint, programme plan, benefits realization plan and benefit profiles are consistent and able to deliver the business case and remain aligned
	Developing the resource management strategy and deployment of the plan
	Developing the monitoring and control strategy and its deployment
	Establishing and managing the appropriate governance arrangements for the programme and its projects
	Ensuring that key programme documentation is current
	Creating and issuing of project briefs
	Identifying and managing programme dependencies
	Progress reporting to the SRO and the programme board on project, business case, programme plan and blueprint achievement
	Adjusting the projects dossier, blueprint and plans to optimize benefits realization
	Managing stakeholder expectations and participating in communications activities to inform stakeholders of progress and issues

Role	Area of focus
Business change manager(s)	Consulting with the programme manager on designing the projects dossier, and scheduling the tranches and constituent projects to ensure that the transition will align with the required benefits realization Ensuring that changes are implemented in the business Ensuring that the business continues to operate effectively during the period of change Providing adequate and appropriate business and operational resources to the programme and its projects to ensure that outputs are designed, developed and assured to give them the best chance of enabling the scale of improvements required Making sure that operational functions are adequately prepared and ready to change when transition starts Ensuring that plans are in place to maintain business operations during the change process until transition and handover is complete; also providing input to the reviews Planning the transition within operational areas, accommodating requirements to maintain business operations Ensuring that the focus remains once transition is completed, to establish the new ways of working and ensure that old practices do not creep back
Programme office	Supporting the development of planning, control and information management arrangements Gathering information and presenting progress reports on projects Supporting the programme manager in the development of reports Providing the programme teams with information and resources that can assist with the design of documentation Establishing and operating the programme's information and configuration management systems, procedures and standards Collecting monitoring and measurement data and keeping the information up to date Collecting and presenting information on business performance Ensuring that there are coherent and common project-level standards in place for all document management arrangements for the programme

9 The business case

9 The business case

'Experience taught me a few things. One is to listen to your gut, no matter how good something sounds on paper. The second is that you're generally better off sticking with what you know. And the third is that sometimes your best investments are the ones you don't make.'
Donald Trump

The business case in programme management is the illustration of the justification to make the change. They come in many different shapes and sizes and there is a danger of a lot of duplication between the contents of the business case and other documents; the approach is often specific to organizations so this advice has to be generic.

Many organizations see business cases as a necessary evil to be able to get at the funding, and the detail is quickly filed away in File 13 (bottom drawer and hidden from sight) and forgotten about, unless it is produced as evidence later to blame or prove the innocence of someone.

Example

A finance director at a programme board meeting made a telling comment: 'How come we seem to spend months getting to the point where I sign the business case, then we hear nothing from the project for 18 months, at which point I'm told it is 18 months behind schedule and about to go over budget?'

This sums up the approach of many organizations to their business case management.

Another reality is that numbers are often created to fit the justifications. Consequently, the benefits are exaggerated and costs minimized to help the numbers stack up so that the business case can get approval to go ahead.

The business case is intended to be a brief summary (compared with the rest of the documentation) of the programme. The content is derived from the other documents which are the result of the preparations carried out in Defining a Programme.

The senior responsible owner (SRO) will use the business case to get approval to continue the programme and start the first tranche. Think of this as a promise. The sponsoring group agrees to make available the resources required because the SRO promises to deliver defined changes and associated benefits. You and the BCM are responsible for this preparation. If you do a poor job in Defining a Programme the business case might be a summary of rubbish. Your boss, the SRO, might then make a promise that he/she can't keep. Not a good career move for you!

'Statistics are used much like a drunk uses a lamppost: for support, not illumination.'
Vin Scully

9.1 BASIC PRINCIPLES

There are four parts to the business case. Firstly, there are the **options** that have been identified. One of them should always be 'do nothing'. For example, if you are running a compliance programme, this will give you the justification to change (i.e. avoidance of the penalties for not changing). There should always be at least three reasonable options for the SRO to consider, which means that at least three potential blueprints will need to be developed to enable the analysis.

Secondly, there are the **benefits**. These have been covered extensively in the benefits management chapter (Chapter 5) and this chapter will focus on the concept of risk-factoring the benefits to ensure they are realistic.

Thirdly, there are the **costs**. The different blueprints will have different delivery paths and in fact a preferred blueprint may also have a number of delivery options. The business case should include the costs for each of these and the associated level of risks with the estimates. The majority of the costs are associated with the projects.

Fourthly, there are the **risks**: some options will have more risk than others. There may be some parts of the desired change that will yield modest benefits with high risk: you might want to consider culling these.

Overall the balance between benefits versus cost (see Figure 9.1), time and risk is fundamental to business case choices and decisions.

The business case often evolves during the programme. It shouldn't be a document that is created at the end of programme definition to sell the justification for expenditure (which happens in many organizations). It is a concept that evolves through a number of documents (see Figure 9.2). The programme mandate provides the strategic concept, the programme brief sets out the justification to continue with the work and finally the full business case is produced.

The decision about the right course of action will be based on risk to the organization and the chances of success. The lower-risk approach often produces the lower benefits, but you can't have it all ways.

Once approved, the key review points are at the ends of tranches, when the viability is reassessed and decisions are made to either continue, change direction or stop.

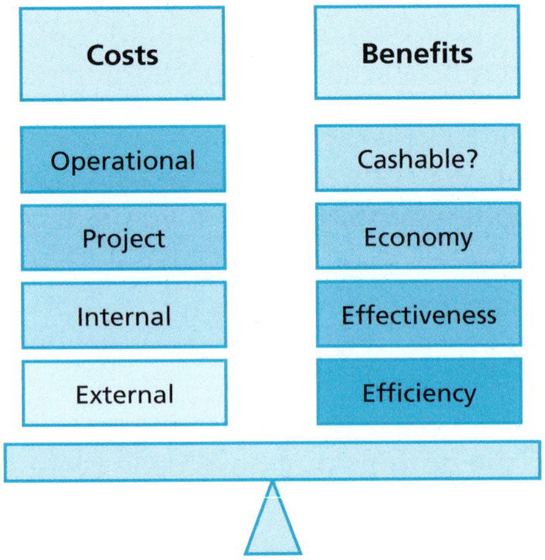

Figure 9.1 Balance of costs and benefits

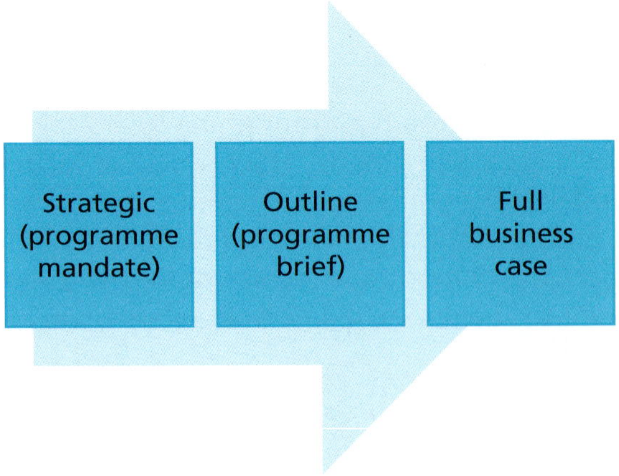

Figure 9.2 Development of the business case

9.2 WHAT DOES MSP HAVE TO SAY?

In MSP the business case provides the vital test of the viability of the programme. It answers the question: 'Is the investment in this programme still worth it?' It evolves from the early documents (e.g. programme mandate and programme brief), and develops throughout the lifecycle, providing a critical decision-making tool.

It provides more than just the basis for initial approval to start the programme. It is actively maintained throughout the programme, and continually updated with new information on benefits, costs and risks.

The business case presents the optimum 'mix' of information used to judge whether or not the programme is (and remains) desirable, viable and achievable.

Developing and maintaining the business case includes:

- Genesis of the business case as it gains detail from initial elements in the original programme mandate, to outline business case in the programme brief and then a full business case that is updated as the programme proceeds.
- The business case construction that sets out costs, the benefits realization and the risk profiles, to assess programme viability.

Reviewing the business case should be an ongoing activity by the programme manager, business change manager (BCM) and programme office. It should also be formally validated (reviewed and re-accepted) at the end of each tranche by the programme board and SRO.

Managing the business case is important as a check to what extent the programme can realize the expected benefits, and whether changes to the cost benefit profile would alter the status and relative priority of the programme in relation to meeting the corporate strategic objectives.

Table 9.1 shows costs that should be considered for inclusion in the business case.

9.3 WHAT DOES THIS MEAN TO YOU?

The business case is a rather dangerous document for you, and it reflects the difference in roles between yourself and the BCMs. You organize the work that consumes most of the money. You have to deliver the means for the organization to change. The BCMs actually change the way operational work is done to bring about improvements that realize enough benefits. Together you produce the return on investment. It's a partnership, so you should be clear what you are signing up for.

9.3.1 What do you need to do?

> *'There are two ways of lying. One, not telling the truth and the other, making up statistics.'*
> Josefina Vazquez Mota

This quotation can be summarized by saying get your facts straight and make sure you can stand behind the numbers in the business case in relation to the cost of change.

The programme business case will be based on the aggregated costs of the projects and should include the cost of the programme overhead. As the programme proceeds each project will work to its allotted budget. A project in a programme doesn't usually need to have a separate business case.

It is undoubtedly true that if business cases included the full cost of the organizational change then many of the failures that have happened would never have proceeded. Even the cost of the business change team will be challenged in immature organizations.

Table 9.1 Costs to include in the business case

Type	Description	Possible information source
Project costs, sometimes referred to as investment or development costs	Project costs in acquiring and delivering the enabling outputs For project and programme contingency and change budget	Projects dossier Programme plan Project business cases
Benefits realization costs	Setting up and implementing measurement, monitoring, and reporting on benefits realization Other costs incurred in achieving the benefits, which can be attributed to benefits – for example, compensation packages for staff	Benefits management strategy Benefit profiles Benefits realization plan
Business change and transition costs	Cost of preparing, training, moving and supporting an operational unit until new practices are embedded. This could include interim operational resources required to embed the change Costs of activities defined in the Realizing the Benefits element of the tranche, including the costs of the BCM and business change team	Programme plan Resource management plan Benefit profiles
Programme management costs	Some programme roles will be full time: for example the programme office and the programme manager Associated costs for these roles and for programme management activities: for example office space, programme tools for tracking and reporting progress Contingency budget for dealing with risk and change Assurance and review costs	Resource management plan Information management strategy Programme communications plan Quality and assurance strategy Programme plan
Capital costs	Capital costs are normally for fixed assets, which can often be found under the 'technology' heading in the blueprint. In accountancy terms the impact of these costs will often be spread over a number of years	Blueprint

Example

In 2007, Aspire Europe worked with a client to calculate the true cost of project delivery. It was found that the costs of 45 dedicated staff were accounted for in the business cases but research on what resources were actually being used showed that more than 150 days per month were being consumed by using operational resources that were not accounted for. In effect, two-thirds of the resources being used were not in the business cases and this helped to explain why the organization was struggling, as its response was to bring in more project people who promptly pulled in more operational staff to help.

There are areas which are often overlooked; these are some examples:

- Risk contingency is often non-existent or minimal, sometimes due to inexperience, sometimes for cultural reasons. But things may not work out as expected and it will cost money to put them right.
- Stakeholder engagement and communications are important: they take time to do well and they are not free.
- There is often significant quality work over and above what is done in projects.
- As transition occurs and the benefits are realized there may be hidden costs in terms of maintenance, warranties and different working practices.

These need to be systematically identified and included in the business case.

Hints and tips

The SRO is accountable for delivering the business case; he/she is your boss. As you monitor progress constantly ask yourself what is the impact on the business case. This will increase your chance of making your boss successful.

If costs are put out of scope to improve the business case, ensure that they are being picked up elsewhere, otherwise they will give someone a nasty surprise later.

You are responsible for identifying all the costs. Seek help from financial experts, people who run the organization, back-office specialists. It will be rare if your programme is the first of its kind anywhere. Try to find other similar ones and see if you can learn from them.

Most important of all make sure the business case is realistic. People can always be stretched a little; they can be stretched more for a limited period, but do this for too long and they will either break or walk away. Make sure that estimates for products or people to be bought in are thoroughly prepared. If you get this wrong the suppliers will not stop charging you just because you are running out of budget.

Setting the level of confidence on the costs and the benefits will help you to provide a more balanced and achievable business case. Table 9.2 is a useful tool for evaluating benefits.

9.4 YOUR ROLE AND THE BUSINESS CASE

> *'Most business cases are a work of fiction, the others are either completely naïve or simply fraudulent. I am never quite sure which is which but all are wrong.'* Rod Sowden

The responsibilities for the business case are evenly spread around the programme board, and the interfaces with the other members can be summarized as follows.

You will be under the most pressure to get the project and programme costs down and make the numbers stack up. But make sure the change and benefits stated in the business case are realistic in relation to the time and costs. Once the programme starts to roll you will be focused on budgets and cost tracking. You need to work very closely with the project to support them and also keep an eye out so that there are no short cuts being taken to save money which could undermine the benefits and blueprint.

Table 9.2 Confidence evaluation

Confidence	Value	Explanation of confidence
Very high	90%	This should only be used if the level of certainty is almost total. It will normally only be achieved with low levels of dependency on other initiatives and in areas where there is direct control of events and where this kind of benefit has been delivered in the past in this way.
Highly likely	75%	This should be used where there is previous experience of achieving a benefit of this kind in this context. There may be areas of ambiguity, possibly with stakeholder commitment, or a small number of dependencies outside the control of the initiative that may affect the total value of the benefits.
Likely	60%	Likely is when, on the balance of probabilities, most of the benefit will be achieved. Under the management controls there will be a number of factors that could be positive or could be negative, one of which may be previous experience of delivering this type of change into particular areas. The amount of value attributed reflects the element of uncertainty and what you can be sure will actually turn up. This doesn't mean that the outstanding amount of the estimate will not appear, but it is a case of being prudent.
Uncertain	40%	This is where the management controls are highlighting that there are recognized risks to achieving the benefit. These could be for a number of reasons and it reflects your confidence in the ability of the organization to deliver the change and capture the benefits. It may also reflect high levels of negative effects that could undermine the positive benefits. Where the benefit is 'uncertain' it may highlight that additional effort is required to leverage the opportunity over and above the work of the normal projects and programme team – this effort may not be available or its effectiveness may be limited.
Low likelihood	20%	A low likelihood rating may well reflect that the potential benefit has high levels of ambiguity associated with it, which reduces confidence that the value can be delivered. This may be reflected in a very high-value benefit which is going to require large-scale organizational change to achieve or may face significant resistance. This will increase the costs and threats to business performance to gain the prize.

You are responsible for most of the preparation work in Defining a Programme, from which the business case is derived. While the SRO will sign it off, if it all goes badly wrong who do you think will get the blame?

9.4.1 Business change manager

With the BCMs who will have their names against the benefits, some may be spread across different parts of the organization and some may be unique to a specific area. The big thing is that you are clear on what each BCM is signing up to and they have clear line of sight on how and when this will be delivered.

9.4.2 Senior responsible owner

With the SRO you will need to be transparent and honest. This is the one document on which their performance will be judged. They will want it to be realistic but if the numbers don't stack up they will probably put you under pressure to reassess your costs: this is just an inevitable part of the process. Remember that if you take costs out of the business case they won't disappear, so you will have a difficult communications job to do to your organization if this happens.

9.4.3 Project teams

Unless you have an emergent programme, projects will not exist when the first business case is prepared. As you start projects you need to allocate budget. The programme plans and estimates will provide a summary: the project will develop their own more detailed plans. Make sure their scope doesn't creep as they do this.

Table 9.3 shows the MSP areas of focus for the key roles.

Table 9.3 Areas of focus for the key roles in the business case

Role	Area of focus
Senior responsible owner (SRO)	Answering to the sponsoring group for the successful delivery of the programme and achievement of the business case
	Securing investment for the programme
	Ensuring that the business case is controlled and audit trails are in place to account for changes as the programme develops
	Scanning the business horizons surrounding the programme for issues that will lead to realignment of the programme in some way
	Ensuring that the progress of the programme remains aligned with the business case
	Consulting with the sponsoring group to identify any early-warning indicators of change that may undermine the business case or cause it to lose strategic alignment
	Initiating independent assurance reviews of business case viability
Programme manager	Preparing the business case
	Supporting the SRO in the ongoing validation and review of the business case
	Managing the programme's expenditure against the overall investment defined in the business case
	Identifying opportunities to optimize the business case
Business change manager(s)	Profiling the benefits and dis-benefits and their associated costs
	Ensuring that benefits continue to be valid through regular business case reviews
	Ensuring that the full cost of change is being captured in the business case
	Identifying operational risks to the business case and ensuring that they are controlled
	Measuring benefits at the start of the programme and tracking throughout to inform the net benefits
	Managing business change costs
	Managing benefits realization costs
	Realizing the profiled benefits
Programme office	Supporting the SRO and the programme manager in compiling and updating the business case
	Collecting and maintaining business case information
	Facilitating business case reviews

10 Quality and assurance management

10 Quality and assurance management

> *'The greatest danger in times of turbulence is not the turbulence – it is to act with yesterday's logic.'* Peter Drucker

Assurance can be your guardian angel. If you use it correctly it will keep you out of trouble.

Quality management in a programme is somewhat different from that found in a project, where it is all about testing, compliance and fitness for purpose. At a programme level it is about the quality of the management and the way it interfaces with the environment around it, so it does very much affect you.

The value of assurance has become increasingly recognized in recent years. Research has shown that most programmes and projects that go wrong do so quite early on in their lifecycle, and if this had been spotted then a lot of waste could have been avoided by doing things right and making tough decisions.

> *'Success is the result of perfection, hard work, learning from failure, loyalty, and persistence.'* Colin Powell

10.1 BASIC PRINCIPLES

Quality and assurance management are clearly differentiated within MSP; however, they are complementary topics, which is why they are considered together.

Quality management looks at how well the programme is being run, and within an MSP programme there are three dimensions: principles, quality and assurance (see Figure 10.1).

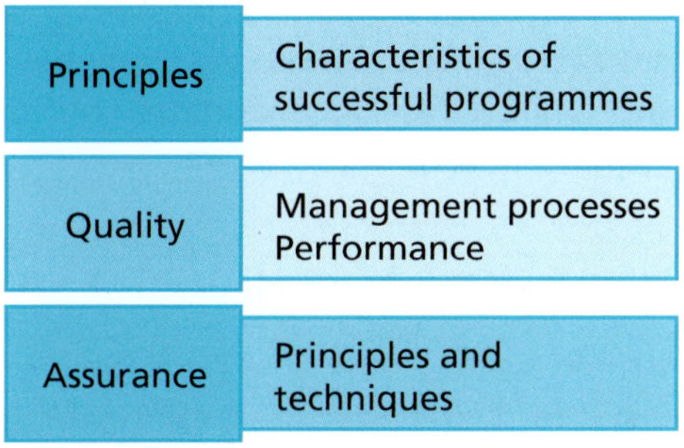

Figure 10.1 The three dimensions of quality management in MSP

Earlier the seven programme management principles that represent the characteristics of successful programmes were explained (see section 1.6.1). Quality management is about making sure that your programme adheres to those principles.

The qualities of the management processes that keep the programme under control are critical to success. If they are too heavy they will not be followed and if they are too light there will be inadequate control: each organization is different. The governance themes identify a number of these qualities in the strategies, but there are a few others that need to be considered. In particular: how well is the team managed, rewarded and the skills and capability built and maintained; how strong and effective is the leadership; and how well is the supply chain managed, maintained and used to the programme's advantage.

Assurance is a regular activity by independent people whose aim is to provide advice and guidance on how you are performing and advice on ways to optimize the achievement of programme objectives or help to resolve problems. Assurance could be provided by an external expert, peer group or governance body; they will review one or more aspects of the programme. The two main advantages for you are that you get help to spot problems (past and future) that you may have missed, and it allows you to give more confidence to the programme board.

10.2 WHAT DOES MSP HAVE TO SAY?

The purpose of quality and assurance management is to ensure that all management aspects of the programme are working appropriately and that it stays on target to achieve its objectives. If a programme does not apply quality and assurance effectively to its management activities, then it is less likely to achieve its objectives and deliver the anticipated value and benefits.

Quality and assurance are defined as follows:

- **Quality** is the totality of features and inherent or assigned characteristics of a product, person, process, service and/or system that bears on its ability to show that it meets expectations or stated needs, requirements or specifications.
- **Assurance** is the systematic set of actions necessary to provide confidence to the senior responsible owner (SRO) and stakeholders that the programme remains under control and on track to deliver and that it is aligned with the organization's strategic objectives.

Quality and assurance management must run continuously throughout the life of a programme; achieving the right level of quality must be an integral part of all the day-to-day activities of the programme.

The programme management principles describe the characteristics of a successful programme and act as critical success factors that apply to all programmes. Therefore, application of and adherence to the principles is essential for the programme to achieve a successful conclusion. To this end, the principles act as the focal point for establishing the critical things that the programme must do to be successful, and quality management makes sure that the programme is doing the right things to assure their achievement.

Whereas the programme principles set out the areas that are critical to the success of a programme, the scope of quality is broader. It covers eight process areas that require management review of their effectiveness in supporting the achievement of the programme objectives (see Figure 10.2).

A number of these processes are covered as part of the MSP governance themes and associated strategies; however, these are areas of particular importance that can cut across a number of themes and strategies, which is why they are being emphasized here in their own right. This is not an exhaustive list, but it provides useful scope for setting out the programme strategy for quality.

The emphasis is on management for all the topics, because good management requires good processes to be in place. The one exception is programme leadership, which is relevant across all the management areas.

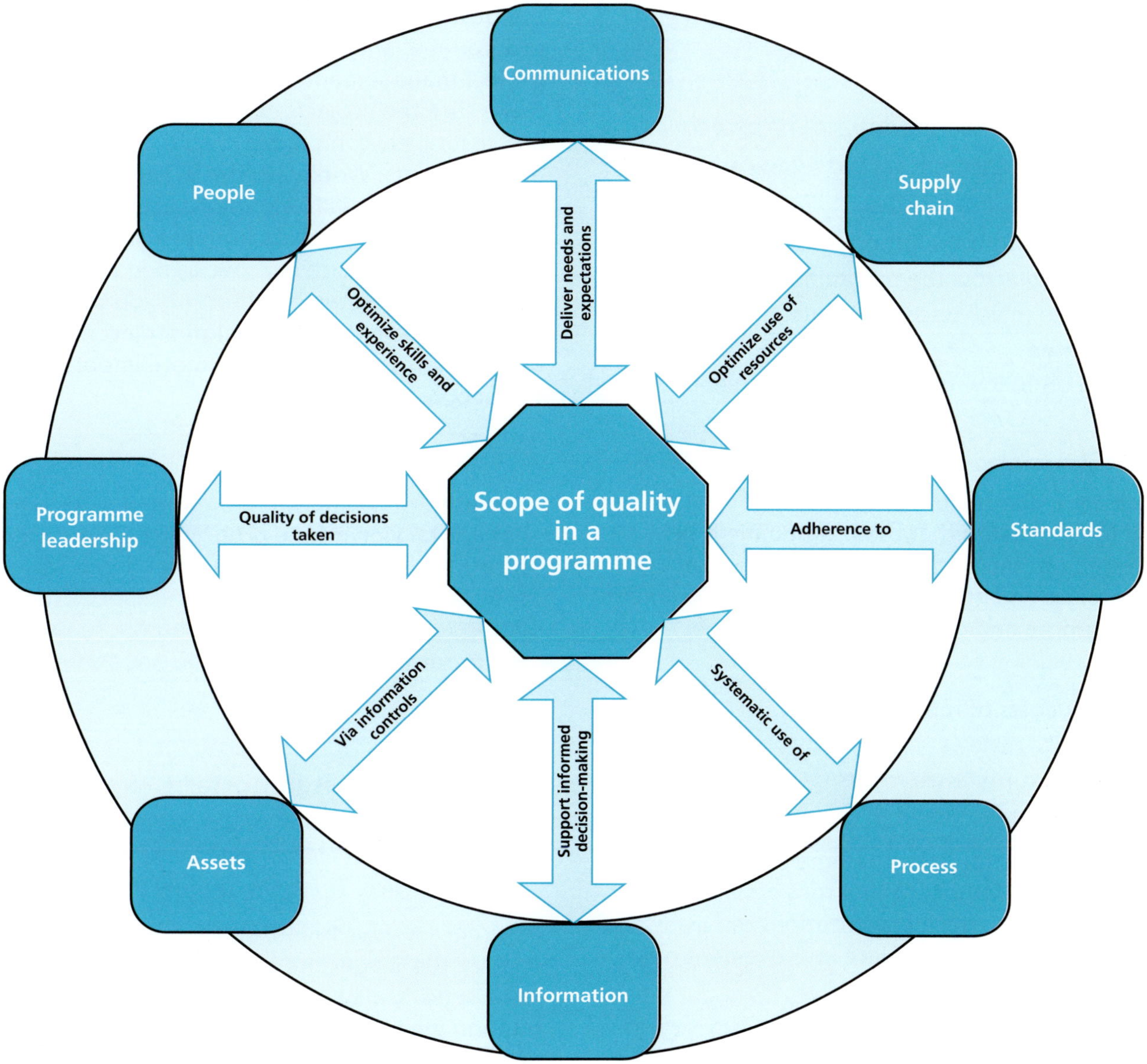

Figure 10.2 Scope of quality in a programme

10.2.1 Assurance management in a programme

10.2.1.1 Assurance management principles

Assurance management should follow an approach that is:

- Independent of the programme
- Integrated across the programme
- Linked to major decision points
- Risk-based
- Based on follow-up action and intervention.

10.2.1.2 Assurance management techniques

There are a number of techniques that can be used to help assure that the programme is being delivered optimally: that is to say in the most appropriate and effective way for the achievement of its purpose and objectives. These include:

- Audit
- Effectiveness of measurements
- Assurance reviews
- P3M3 maturity assessments
- Gated reviews.

P3M3 is the Portfolio, Programme and Project Management Maturity Model that provides a framework with which organizations can assess their performance and put in place improvement plans.

10.3 WHAT DOES THIS MEAN TO YOU?

Your responsibilities, to some extent, cover all aspects of the programme. Others will look after some parts more closely: the business change managers (BCMs) for benefits, the projects for outputs. But it is you who must assess that state of the whole programme. You probably have the best overall knowledge of the projects in the programme, and you should have considerable project management experience. You must make sure the projects embed suitable quality and assurance, compatible with the programme arrangements. Work with the BCMs to establish procedures that will help them verify that they are going to get outputs from the project that will enable operations to improve as needed. As well as thinking beyond technical testing you should think in broader terms than technical project outputs. Just as important, and sometimes more important, are the people aspects.

Hints and tips

You are the one person who from day to day has a total view of the programme; make sure you have confidence in what the BCMs, projects, corporate functions and specialists are doing for the programme so you can reassure the programme board that you are on track to success.

10.3.1 Why is it important to you?

> *'The medical version of programme management: The surgery perfectly followed best practice. The patient sadly died.'* Geoff Reiss

Assurance is your friend, and the less experienced you are the bigger the friends you need. There are some specific areas where you can easily be caught out and where it would be sensible to make use of assurance. Assurance is also important to other roles, particularly the SRO and the BCMs. Use it to give them confidence that you are managing the programme well, or if there are problems to help them understand where and why refinements are needed.

You are responsible for delivering capability in what is probably a complex environment. Your enthusiasm and ambition for this change may not be matched by others. Although they may be nodding and agreeing with everything you say, you need to be assured that when you are being told that plans are in place and progress is going well, that this is actually the case.

Reviews of the projected outputs of the projects and how they align with the blueprint are equally important. It is often the case that minor deviations and changes to specifications at the project level combine to undermine elements of the blueprinted outcomes. The result of this is that some fundamental capabilities may be missing, creating significant problems during transition and undermining the ability to release benefits due to functional deficiencies in the capability.

10.3.2 What do you need to do?

The important thing for the programme manager is to be proactive and ensure that you plan for assurance.

If you have doubts about what is going on in other parts of the organization or the quality and timeliness of the capabilities being developed then you have a justification for instigating assurance reviews so that you know the extent of the issues, or whether you have been worryingly unnecessarily. Request for an assurance review can come from others who may be concerned: the SRO or BCMs for example. This can be a good way to satisfy their concerns and give them confidence. However, remember that assurance reviews can consume significant time and money, so don't use them for every expression of concern.

> **Hints and tips**
>
> Make sure that every review helps you to answer the question: 'Do I now have more or less confidence that the programme is on track to success?'

10.3.3 Assurance approaches

There are a few useful techniques around that cover this. Three of them, all of which represent a form of assurance, are described below.

Health checks are targeted reviews of the whole of a programme, a particular perspective or the performance of a particular group. A health check will need to be scoped and resourced and is intended to be a low-impact method of checking that things are being done in the best way.

Maturity assessments look at the whole or part of an organization in terms of maturity of process. These are not normally used for a single programme but look at how consistently all the programmes are run: without consistency it is difficult to improve. Most are based on the five-level Capability Maturity Model Integration (CMMI):

- **Level 1** Awareness of process – ad hoc, chaotic or heroic, but every one is different.
- **Level 2** Repeatable – some are working to a common plan, but others aren't.
- **Level 3** Defined – all programmes are being managed consistently.
- **Level 4** Managed – they are learning from experience and continually improving.
- **Level 5** Optimized – there are embedded behaviours and practices that are continually improving.

A maturity assessment can be useful within a programme where there are many projects running, so they can be tested for consistency. Where many areas are going through change, a change maturity assessment can check that the lessons are being learned and there is a consistent approach. Level 3 is a good place to be for most organizations.

Gated reviews are often approached with trepidation as they are auditing progress. They are also your best friend because they will identify issues you may not know about. They are a very good place to confess your sins or concerns and share doubts, as the reports are normally non-attributable, but you might want to check that before saying too much.

Good assurance reviews will examine progress so far, and assess the likelihood of the desired outcome and benefits being achieved if the programme proceeds as planned.

> **Hints and tips**
>
> Assurance reviews and maturity assessments are simply mirrors so you can see what you look like through the eyes of others. If you don't like what you see, don't blame the mirror manufacturer for your looks!

10.3.4 Quality strategy and plan

What you produce in the quality and assurance strategy will establish the governance that is described in it. You will produce the quality and assurance plan. It is important you involve others in this work, in particular the project teams and the BCMs (see Figure 10.3).

10.3.4.1 Quality and assurance strategy

As with the other strategies, the core content is summarized in Chapter 2, but here are the specific areas that you will need to cover:

- How assurance of operational areas' readiness for change will be managed
- How you will measure the achievement of the MSP principles
- What assurance approach you will take to monitoring the quality of project outputs
- How you will assure the quality of people management and professional development
- What standards the programme will adhere to and how compliance will be measured
- Type, regularity and source of the assurance reviews: your organization may have a gate process you have to work with
- How maturity assessment will be used to improve project performance (P3M3)
- Relationships with governance groups that may need to review assurance reports: e.g. key stakeholders or customers
- Any specific events that would automatically trigger an audit or review
- Specialist organizations that will be commissioned to undertake technical reviews.

The quality and assurance plan should be developed to cover the whole of the programme lifecycle with the information management strategy linked to it. Good information is critical to programme success and therefore a critical input to quality and assurance.

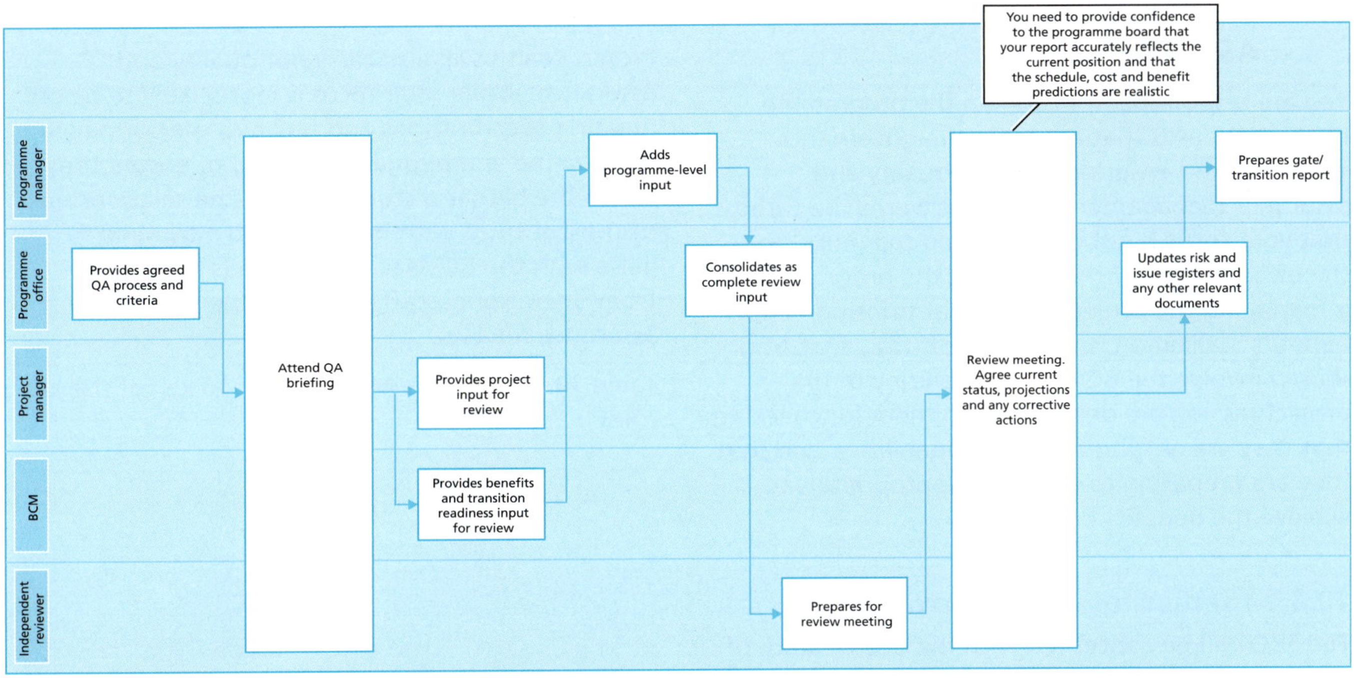

Figure 10.3 Example of the quality and assurance process as preparation for a gate decision point

10.3.4.2 Information management strategy

This strategy can easily be integrated with others. Programmes thrive on information: it is essential for decision-making and, as such, having robust information controls to ensure that decisions are being made based on the right information at the right time is a big responsibility that falls to you.

Here are the specific topics that you should consider:

- Naming conventions for documentation to cover version controls
- Security levels and details around how different levels are controlled
- Information security compliance standards that apply to your programme
- Procedures for checking the integrity of the information being supplied: e.g. highlight reports
- Approved storage and repository arrangements for the information: e.g. shared areas etc.
- How access to different levels of information security will be managed
- How information flows will be checked: e.g. business performance information
- Configuration management procedures and processes
- Explanation of the different templates that should be used and when
- Approach to reviewing and improving information quality.

10.4 YOUR ROLE IN QUALITY AND ASSURANCE

You are responsible for running the programme to the standards that are set in the governance strategies and ensuring that the quality and assurance management plan is delivered. Be careful that your focus is not concentrated too much on the effectiveness of the way that the programme is managing the projects, such that transition and benefits realization is a little bit off the radar. You should involve the BCMs in the scrutiny of the projects as you are dependent on them for checking that they are getting the right capabilities, and that they are preparing to use them appropriately to achieve the benefits.

10.4.1 Senior responsible owner

The SRO will be concerned with the overall state of the programme and whether it is going to meet its objectives. There is often more focus on the projects and whether the money is being spent on the right things in the right places. More enlightened SROs will have their eye on benefits and change management, so it is important that you have a transparent relationship with them and they know the issues you are facing and the potential opportunities.

10.4.2 Business change managers

The BCMs will be dependent on their changes happening in the right way and at the right time, and will need assurance from you that the programme is on track to deliver this. You will be dependent on them for preparation and enacting transitions, then supporting and measuring the realization of benefits. You will need independent assurance that they are doing this well.

10.4.3 Project teams

Project teams will also carry out quality and assurance. While their focus is more likely to be on meeting specifications and technical performance within time and budget, you need to ensure they retain the bigger picture through the relationship of their outputs with benefits. You may need to liaise with the BCMs so that projects have input from operational staff as part of their quality and assurance reviews.

Table 10.1 shows the MSP areas of focus for the key roles.

Table 10.1 Areas of focus for the key roles in quality and assurance management

Role	Area of focus
Senior responsible owner (SRO)	Consults with sponsoring group on approach to programme assurance Ensures that an adequate assurance regime is in place for all aspects of quality in the programme Signs off the quality and information management strategies Initiates assurance reviews and audits Maintains focus on the programme management principles
Programme manager	Develops and implements the quality and assurance strategy, and then plans and coordinates delivery of outputs from the projects that are fit for the purpose of achieving the desired outcomes and benefits Develops and implements the information management strategy and plan Initiates assurance reviews of project and supplier performance Ensures that lessons learned are implemented
Business change manager(s)	Implements transitioning, realizing and reviewing of benefits from the outputs of the projects Initiates assurance reviews of business performance and change readiness Ensures that business change lessons learned are implemented
Programme office	Establishes and maintains the programme's quality and assurance plan and ensures the establishment of the appropriate audit, assurance and review processes for the programme in accordance with the quality and assurance strategy Establishes and maintains the programme's information management plan and ensures the establishment of the appropriate audit, assurance and review processes for the programme in accordance with the information management strategy Provides information to support assurance reviews

PART 2
The transformational flow

11 Introduction to the transformational flow

11 Introduction to the transformational flow

The transformational flow in MSP, which was introduced in Chapter 1 (see Figures 1.3 and 1.4), is the programme lifecycle. This is where all the action happens; the governance themes are active in all the processes, and all the concepts covered in the governance themes come to life.

To help focus your mind on the role of programme manager, in Figure 11.1 some of the process activities have been adjusted to help give you clear and concise advice on where to put your energy. This different view of the lifecycle shows the sequential nature of the processes in the transformational flow.

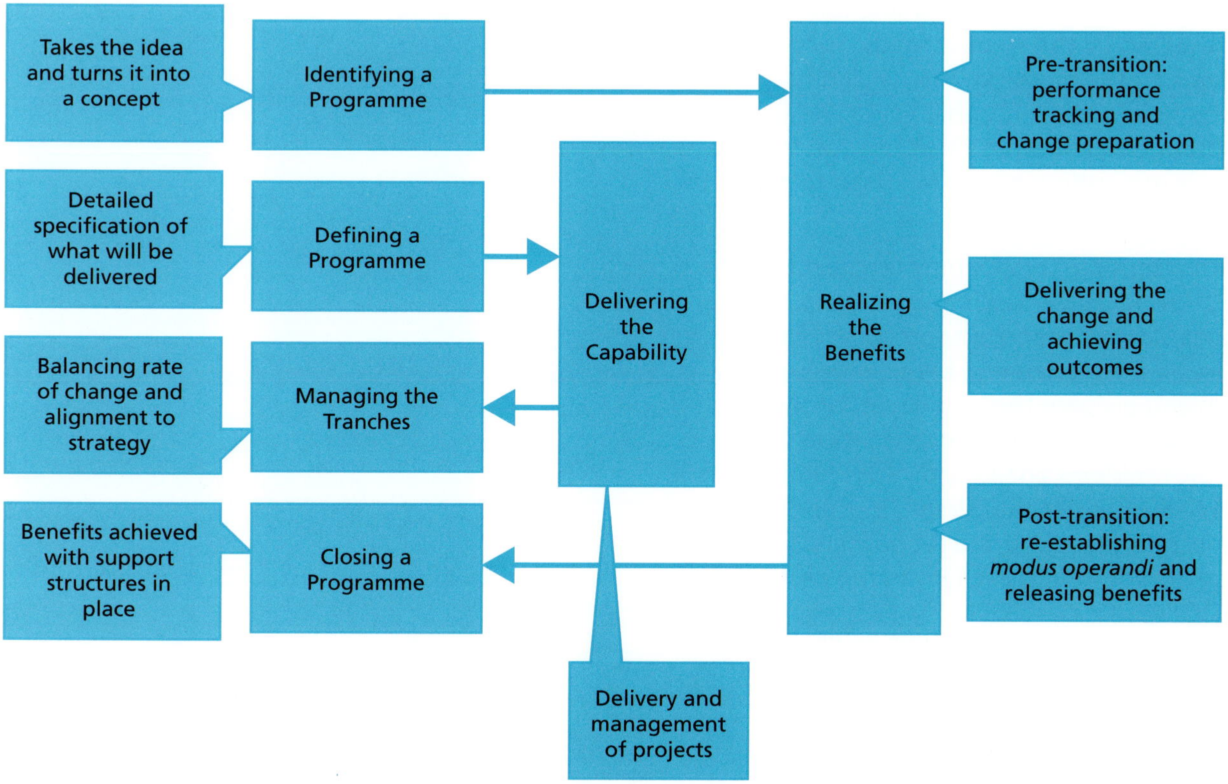

Figure 11.1 Sequential view of the transformational flow

Managing the Tranches is recurrent depending on the number of tranches agreed. Realizing the Benefits runs concurrently throughout the lifecycle and is the main area of focus for the business change manager (BCM). The other processes are largely your domain; you need to work closely with the BCMs on them.

11.1 WHAT DOES THIS MEAN TO YOU?

Think of the transformational flow as the roadmap for the programme. MSP provides a basic roadmap: you must adapt this into a real roadmap that will take the organization to the desired destination – the vision.

The journey through a programme can be a little like travelling by car on busy roads. Sometimes problems on the motorway cause significant delay and you need to find another route. Similarly in a programme sometimes the route you initially choose is not optimum and you need to adjust the roadmap.

It is often sensible to plan only the next tranche in detail, having only a summary roadmap for later tranches. As each tranche approaches closure, capture all the lessons and knowledge you can to help you prepare the best route for the next tranche. In our cars, satellite navigation warns us of traffic problems ahead and offers an alternative route. Sadly it is not that simple in a programme. You must do the job of the sat nav: everyone else will expect you to direct them to the destination successfully.

12 Identifying a Programme

12 Identifying a Programme

> *'Change does not change tradition, it strengthens it. Change is a challenge and an opportunity.'* Prince Philip

You may not yet have been formally appointed as programme manager but you need to be involved in Identifying a Programme as early as possible. There are two things that are important to you:

- Help the senior responsible owner (SRO) to make sure that all members of the sponsoring group have the same understanding about the programme.
- Work hard to gain as much knowledge as you can on the do-ability of the intended changes. Starting with mission impossible means the organization is just taking the first step to failure.

There are many programmes that never come out of the identifying stage because they sort out a vision and, before you know it, there are projects being launched all over the place and the blueprint and benefits go missing. Instead of a programme there is a cluster of projects with no particular context.

Try to make sure that there is a programme brief and there is focus on outcomes and benefits from the start. There must be recognition that you need to go through a formal Defining a Programme process and that the appearance of the programme brief isn't the job done, as so often happens. Don't overlook the programme preparation plan: it will focus attention on what the next stage will involve in terms of resources and outputs, even if you do end up launching early projects.

12.1 WHAT DOES MSP HAVE TO SAY?

Identifying a Programme comprises a number of activities that take an initial or emerging idea or need and frame it into a tangible concept that the business can support through the Defining a Programme process.

12.1.1 Activities

- Sponsor the programme
- Confirm the programme mandate
- Appoint the SRO and programme board
- Produce the programme brief
- Develop the programme preparation plan
- Independent review
- Approval to proceed (with Defining a Programme).

12.2 RECOMMENDED ACTIONS

Here is our specific advice for you on each of the activities. At the outset the programme is likely to have a lot of ambiguity about what is required.

The activities in Identifying a Programme should seek to put context around the programme, clarify its organizational context, outline the vision for the programme and establish a strong team to undertake further development.

The result of these activities may well be a decision not to proceed with the programme: this is OK, as it is much better to stop it early before time and effort are expended on a programme that is unlikely to proceed.

Table 12.1 shows the recommended actions by the programme manager for the activities in this process.

Table 12.1 Recommended actions for the programme manager in Identifying a Programme

Activity	Recommended actions
Develop the programme brief	This is likely to be your first job. It is often the case that in the early days the whole programme will be overdosing on optimism about how great the future will be, so you will need to capture that optimism, but injecting a significant dose of caution will be a good idea. This document isn't definitive. It sets out the strategic direction, so bear this in mind: ■ Vision statement will only be in draft: focus on what the big outcomes will be and why. This is the point where you start thinking about the blueprint. ■ Estimates: they may be finger-in-the-air but think about putting a confidence level with any numbers to show how wild the guess is. ■ Risks should be mainly strategic and business change-related: this is the point where the risk management process starts. ■ Benefits will be largely guesswork at the moment, but this is the point where the benefits process starts. The programme board will sign this off and take ownership of it, as it acts at their terms of reference for the time being; so now you can put together basic terms of references for the individuals as well, or help the SRO to do it.
Develop the programme preparation plan	The existence of the programme preparation plan is essential to ensuring the resources and time are invested in sorting out the blueprint and benefits. This activity is easily overlooked, and if it is, your programme will probably run into trouble because it will bypass the critical business design phase of the programme. So be warned, this is not a 'nice to have': it is essential.
Arrange an independent assurance review	This will most likely be instigated by the SRO, but you should see it as an opportunity to learn from people with more experience and take their advice seriously. In particular, this is also a chance for you to share your concerns about the shape of the programme, especially if there is undue haste to start firing off projects without the benefits and blueprint having been sorted.
Gain authorization to proceed	This is the stop/go decision point, and it is the cheapest point at which to stop. However, with the initial optimism the programme will probably continue. You should have your plans ready to go and mobilize as soon as the SRO gives the all clear.

13

Defining a Programme

13 Defining a Programme

'The rate of change is not going to slow down anytime soon. If anything, competition in most industries will probably speed up even more in the next few decades.' John P. Kotter

You should regard Defining a Programme as one of the most critical parts of the lifecycle: the other is transition. If the options for change are not carefully considered, if plans and governance are rushed, the programme is unlikely to be successful.

From your point of view you can think about Defining a Programme in two parts:

- **Designing the Programme** This will focus on the vision, blueprint and business outcomes, then on the best way to deliver the change.
- **Developing the Programme** This will focus on configuring the governance and on the programme strategies and plans.

By splitting this stage into two parts, you can build in a stop/go decision once the outcomes and direction have been set. This avoids unnecessary planning and preparation for an unacceptable solution.

Hints and tips

This is the stage that will be the most challenging for you if you come from a project background: you will want to crack on – but rush and you will do so at your peril.

13.1 WHAT DOES MSP HAVE TO SAY?

Defining a Programme takes the concept that evolved during Identifying a Programme and develops a compelling business proposition that gains the commitment of the sponsoring group and stakeholders.

The business case and governance for the programme will be developed. The governance defines the strategies for quality, information, stakeholders, risks and issues, benefits, resources, monitoring and control. The various programme approaches contained in the strategies, plans and schedules (covering risk management, communications, benefits realization, resources, quality etc.) are developed to provide information on the resources, dependencies and timescales for delivery and realization of benefits.

A key activity is the development of the blueprint and the investigation of the options available, and the options for delivery.

The inevitable trade-off between resources, costs, quality, timings and benefits requires agreement between the sponsoring group and senior responsible owner (SRO). At the completion of Defining a Programme, formal approval is required from the sponsoring group and SRO to proceed with the programme.

'Proper planning and preparation prevents poor performance.' British Army adage

13.1.1 Activities

- Establish the infrastructure for Defining a Programme
- Establish the team to define the programme
- Identify and analyse the stakeholders
- Refine the vision statement
- Develop the blueprint
- Develop the benefit profiles
- Model and refine the benefits
- Validate the benefits
- Develop the projects dossier
- Identify tranches
- Design the programme organization
- Develop the governance arrangements
- Develop the programme plan
- Consolidate the programme definition
- Develop and confirm the programme business case
- Prepare for the first tranche
- Approval to proceed.

13.2 RECOMMENDED ACTIONS

13.2.1 Designing the Programme

The recommended actions are linked to the modified activities from MSP to reflect the change of skills and experience needed for the different elements.

Table 13.1 shows the recommended actions by the programme manager for this stage.

> **Hints and tips**
>
> This is where the seeds of failure are sown if you do not do a thorough job.

13.2.2 Developing the Programme

Now that you know where you are going, you can start to plan for the delivery in detail. Table 13.2 shows the recommended actions for this stage.

Table 13.1 Recommended actions for the programme manager in Designing the Programme

Activity	Recommended actions
Establish the infrastructure	This may seem trivial but it is surprising just how much irritation, delay and demotivation it causes when people join the programme team and they don't have a desk, phone or computer and can't get anywhere to hold meetings. It is your responsibility to make sure adequate basic infrastructure is in place now.
Establish the team	You should ensure you are clear about your role. You will need help from the business change manager (BCM) who will release time from their normal role to deliver this work. You will need to involve a range of specialists as outlined in Chapter 3. Working out what skills and experience you need is relatively easy; the hard part will be finding the people and getting them freed up from other duties. Ask the SRO to help if you hit a major roadblock getting key critical resource. It is good to establish the right protocols and precedencies early in the programme as problems getting the right resources will occur again and again throughout the lifecycle.
Engage key stakeholders	You may know who some of the stakeholders are; talk to other key roles such as the BCM, the SRO, technical manager etc. to identify the rest. All the stakeholders will have valuable information on their concerns and aspirations. This should be shared with the programme team, and you might want some of the team to validate the stakeholder profiles. You and the BCM are key communications channels, and your profiles and track records should be used to gain the attention of your colleagues and managers.
Refine the vision statement	You should be comfortable that it is understandable by all stakeholders and as motivating as possible. The vision should also provide you with enough context to enable you to develop the blueprint and the benefits. It has been known for people to mistake the vision for a blueprint. Enlist the help of a professional communicator if the programme is higher risk. This is the first major communication product for the programme. You want to make a good impression and establish good communication practice. There will be many more communications to come.
Align existing projects	You will need to do an impact analysis on existing projects in the business areas in scope of the programme. Sacrifices will need to be made but it may be necessary to protect some 'sacred cow' projects in some business areas. If you have a portfolio office you must involve them in this activity as they are likely to have established prioritization procedures in place. Stopping projects is a great way of releasing resources to the programme, but it is also a great way of losing stakeholder support, so tread carefully.
Develop the blueprint	You and the BCMs will be responsible for sourcing a lot of business performance and process information on how things work at the moment. As well as the BCMs you will need to enlist help from a wide range of specialists, including strategic and performance planners. This is where your team-building skills will be needed as there is always a wide range of opinions among specialists. You need to make sure they make sensible and objective choices.

Table continues

Table 13.1 *continued*

Activity	Recommended actions
Develop the benefit profiles	The BCM will need to develop the benefits from the work you did on the blueprint. The assessments must be realistic and achievable; it is better to under-promise and over-deliver. You are likely to be called on to help as you may have more programme management experience and can explain the importance of this work. Make sure that the risks are being captured, particularly those that may reduce the size of the benefit or may be double-counted.
Identify the tranches	If the tranches can be aligned with a strategic business plan commitment or to leverage or avoid certain events, this is the opportunity to do it. You need to look carefully at the benefits opportunities associated with these step changes. You must assume that your programme is not the only initiative making changes in the same business areas. You do not accidentally want to create change overload so find out what else will be in flight during the timeframe of your programme.
Appraise the options	You will be a key player in this; with the help of the BCMs and specialists you need to ensure you balance the needs of the programme with the needs of the operational parts of the business. For example, project and technically oriented people may have a tendency to over-engineer the outputs, perhaps realizing all the benefits but at a cost and timescale that are unacceptable. Conversely operational people might prefer simpler change, which might result in less chaotic transition but will not realize enough benefits. You should be looking to keep your SRO informed of progress and consult them as part of the appraisal process so they are ready to make the decision rather than just presenting them with the options – evolution not revolution.
Decision gateway	You now have a preferred blueprint design, delivery option and benefits analysis. You need to complete a risk assessment of these initial choices. The test is to make sure that the balances between benefits and cost, time and risk are acceptable, and that the emerging business case is in line with the outline business case from the programme brief. You definitely need to discuss this with the SRO and BCMs as you go along. If the programme is looking to be too costly, lengthy or there is too much risk, go to the SRO armed with alternative approaches, less ambitious design in the blueprint and less expensive delivery (projects). If this is not possible, suggest options to reduce the scope of the programme and potential for benefits. If you need to do this, make sure you recommend removing those elements that have a poor benefit return compared with their cost. At this point you should be formalizing the 'stop', 'go' or 'go back and try again' decision by the programme board and the SRO.

Table 13.2 Recommended actions for the programme manager in Developing the Programme

Activity	Recommended actions
Define the projects dossier	You should satisfy yourself and the BCMs that these projects will deliver the capabilities needed for the benefits. You should also be thinking about scheduling non-project activities. Make sure you link the capability and requirements for the projects to the content in the blueprint.
Design the programme organization	It is important that you have eyes and ears in the projects as well as embedded in the operations. This is essential for the intelligence you will need to deliver your objectives. When designing the delivery organization, you need to know what resources you will require for when you move into the tranches.
Develop governance arrangements	It is largely your territory to pull together the governance arrangements consisting of the programme strategies and associated plans. This does not mean you do the work on your own. These arrangements must work for the rest of the programme team, the operational people and the projects, and most importantly, give the SRO and sponsoring group confidence that good controls are being put in place. Therefore you will need to consult people from all these areas.
Develop the programme plans	The programme plan is much more than the projects. It is critical that enough time is allowed for transition and that realistic benefits realization timescales are in place; commitments now will be expected to be kept once you move into delivery. The programme plan provides the backbone: when you have drafted this, you can think about the other plans. All the other plans represent everything else that needs to be done. You might want to consider consolidating all the plans into the programme plan, but if you do this, make sure it is still readable.
Finalize definition documentation including the business case	You will consolidate all the information created so far into a complete set of programme documentation. It is important that good information management is established. All of the documents need to go into configuration management with version control and baselines set. If you don't do this it will be harder to manage changes to the programme later. Check that there is clarity between cashable and non-cashable savings and that current estimates are fully reflected with sensitivity ratings included. You are responsible for compiling this documentation and through it you are recommending that the SRO commits your organization to the programme as defined.

Table continues

Table 13.2 *continued*

Activity	Recommended actions
Prepare for first tranche	You will now have to assign the resources needed to start the first projects, and you should check that the BCM will allocate the resources to join the change team. The infrastructure established for this work in Defining a Programme may need to be expanded to cater for the project teams and the change team. While this is actually done at the start of the first tranche it is wise to prepare for it now. You do not want to get the go-ahead from the sponsoring group to find you cannot start anything yet because people have nowhere to work.
Arrange an independent review	Despite your best endeavours and diligent work so far, you have been close to the work in Defining a Programme and it is easy for you to miss something or make assumptions subconsciously. An independent review can be invaluable and allow you to make any last-minute refinements. This does not need to be a costly formal review: sometimes having an experienced colleague spend half a day walking through the work completed so far can be quite revealing.
Decision gate: stop, go or go back	Hopefully you are now moving into delivery and the programme is under way; this is where you have to live up to all the promises in the strategies, plans and benefit forecasts.

14

Managing the Tranches

14 Managing the Tranches

> *'Culture does not change because we desire to change it. Culture changes when the organization is transformed – the culture reflects the realities of people working together every day.'* Frances Hesselbein

Managing the Tranches consists of the process and activities which keep the balance between the rate of potential change being delivered by projects and the ability of the organization to absorb that change.

The activities are designed to ensure that controls are in place and working. They also focus on ensuring that the programme remains aligned with the organization's strategic direction.

Major problems with projects and benefits realization are managed at this level; this is where you will escalate issues that arise in your own domain and oversee the resolution via the programme board or higher.

14.1 WHAT DOES MSP HAVE TO SAY?

The purpose of the Managing the Tranches process is to implement the defined programme management governance strategies for the programme, ensure that the capability delivery is aligned with the strategic direction of the organization, and enable the release of benefits. This accepts that, as the programme progresses, it will need to be adapted and refined to ensure the effective delivery of the tranches and the final outcomes.

A key principle of the Managing the Tranches process is to maintain the balance between the rate of change being offered by the Delivering the Capability process and the rate of change that the operational areas can cope with. This is managed through the Realizing the Benefits stage, which aligns the programme with the evolving and changing strategic needs of the organization.

Hints and tips

If you have designed your governance well and have well-developed delegated authority, then your life will be a lot easier.

Unlike some of the activities in other processes, which tend to happen in a logical sequence, the activities in Managing the Tranches may recur or happen concurrently. Most of the activities are linked to the governance themes and are intended to trigger the cycles. For example, you do not 'manage risk and issues' once: this is a day-to-day activity that occurs throughout the tranche.

14.1.1 Activities

- Establish the tranche
- Direct work
- Manage risks and issues
- Control and deliver communications
- Initiate compliance audits
- Maintain alignment between programme blueprint and business strategy objectives
- Maintain information and asset integrity

- Manage people and other resources
- Manage procurement and contracts
- Monitor, report and control
- Execute transition and maintain stable operations
- Prepare for next tranche
- Close tranche.

14.2 RECOMMENDED ACTIONS

Table 14.1 shows the recommended actions by the programme manager for the activities in this process.

Table 14.1 Recommended actions for the programme manager in Managing the Tranches

Activity	Recommended actions
Establish the programme delivery team	You will now need to establish the programme organization designed and approved during Defining the Programme. Roles need to be allocated to chosen people and they need to be briefed. If some of these people have limited experience of programme management you will need to make arrangements to develop their competencies. The team is expanding so there is more team-building work for you to do. There will need to be a development plan for the team; this could be training or coaching – it will depend on the situation.
Establish the governance control framework	You have been responsible for putting together the programme strategies and associated plans. You probably know more about them than anyone else at this stage. Everyone with a governance-related role will need to be briefed and sometimes trained so that they can carry out their work according to the procedures and rules approved. Governance-related roles are those who will make decisions and others who will report to and advise the decision makers.
Mobilize project delivery	What happens next is embedded in the approved plans. You need to communicate, instruct and explain to everyone assigned an activity in a plan that needs to start now. You will be mainly focused on preparing to start projects and controlling the early starters. You need to work with the BCMs to involve them in project start-up as they or their colleagues will be represented on project boards. It is also time for them to get their work under way.
Manage programme governance framework	How this is done is defined in the programme strategies. There may be some people who are new to programme work and you should be supporting and coaching them. Don't be shy of doing this even if some of these people are very senior executives. Get the SRO to help if they unreasonably reject your offers of help. You will oversee, coordinate, track, report and advise on a range of activities, so you will need to ensure your programme office team operate like a well-oiled machine and do not give the appearance of being a bureaucratic overhead that is slowing things down: a weak team will be sluggish whereas a good team will increase the agility.

Activity	Recommended actions
Manage transition and business performance	While the transition and stable operation activity is the responsibility of the BCMs you are likely to be asked to help. The BCMs are likely to have a much closer understanding of operations but may not be as experienced as you at planning and other such skills needed to manage transition. A key consideration is the information being used to measure performance. It is worthwhile checking the accuracy and how current it is: big decisions will be made about this data so it needs to be right, and the programme office is the source.
Review and refine the programme direction	This will be your opportunity to flag up concerns you may have about the realism of the approach and, in particular, any concerns you may have regarding the delivery of capabilities, the realization of benefits and level of business change being planned. If the blueprint is proving unachievable or the benefits can't be delivered, now is the time to speak up. If you do this make sure you go armed with suggested solutions as well as problems.
Review and refine the programme governance framework	As you approach the end of the first tranche the governance arrangements have been used for some time. Some parts will work better than others. The programme may need to change direction. This is the time for you to gather together all the lessons learned and propose refinements to improve governance for the next tranches. This repeats at the end of every tranche except the last one.
End-of-tranche assurance review	This is best conducted independently as part of your quality and assurance plan. The lessons learned so far are not limited to refining governance. You need to judge whether the delivery of capabilities, their transition into operational use and the benefits that have resulted are in line with expectations. Remember, most programmes have lots of uncertainties, and assumptions made early on need to be tested now. The next tranche may need to be adjusted to account for what you have learned. The assurance should review the governance and viability of direction of the programme from the previous two activities.
Decision gate	Once the assurance review is completed you should be seeking sponsoring group approval for the next tranche; if you don't get it then the programme will move to close.

15 Delivering the Capability

15 Delivering the Capability

'The world hates change, yet it is the only thing that has brought progress.' Charles Kettering

Without doubt, this is your stamping ground as delivering capability is your job. The process can start very early once Defining a Programme is complete. As soon as you have projects rolling then this process is in place and operating.

Even though this is a major area for you, don't underestimate the role of the business change managers (BCMs): they are the customers for what you are producing, so they should be putting people onto project boards, signing off the requirements and ensuring that the capability delivers what they need to release the benefits.

15.1 WHAT DOES MSP HAVE TO SAY?

The Delivering the Capability process covers the activities for coordinating and managing project delivery according to the programme plan. Delivery from the projects dossier provides the new outputs that enable the capabilities described in the blueprint. The activities of Delivering the Capability are repeated for each tranche of the programme.

This process delivers the capability defined in the blueprint through the projects specified in the projects dossier. The detail in the blueprint provides the input requirements for the projects, which adopt the strategic requirements and undertake detailed specification and design to deliver the outputs that create the capability needed to achieve the outcomes and deliver the benefits.

Hints and tips

This process is probably your comfort zone, but don't get too cosy because it is only part of your new job.

15.1.1 Activities

- Start projects
- Engage stakeholders
- Align projects with benefits realization
- Align projects with programme objectives
- Governance: manage and control delivery:
  - Monitor and control progress
  - Manage risks and control issues
- Close projects.

15.2 RECOMMENDED ACTIONS

This process is the one which covers the launch, control and delivery of the projects within the programme.

The programme-level activities are relatively light touch and the main controls are within the project management method (which is defined in the monitoring and control strategy). Table 15.1 shows the recommended actions by the programme manager for this process.

Table 15.1 Recommended actions for the programme manager in Delivering the Capability

Activity	Recommended actions
Start projects	It is your responsibility to kick off the projects, so documents such as the blueprint and programme plan will be important inputs and provide the context for briefing the project teams. A lot of preparatory work should already be complete for each project as part of the projects dossier, so you can consider skipping some of the early activities in project processes: for example 'Starting up a Project' as in PRINCE2. Projects will report to you and through you to the programme board. The level of governance for each project will depend on size and risk. You and the BCM will need to work together to appoint the project executive, but you are responsible for the project manager. The project executive (sponsor) will be accountable for the project to the programme board. You need to choose carefully who you appoint as a good working relationship between you is critical. You should involve the BCMs in the appointment of the board: they may want to provide operational representation, e.g. senior user as in PRINCE2. Operations should be involved in all projects as they proceed. They need to be sure they are going to get new capabilities that will enable them when in use to achieve sufficient performance improvements to realize the benefits required. It is important that operations are engaged rather than just informed, because that will cause resistance and they will act like victims!
Align project with the programme	There are two parts to this: ■ Align project with blueprint and benefits ■ Align project with programme objectives. As projects are started they need to be briefed on how they will contribute to parts of the blueprint, and through their outputs to benefits realization. As projects progress further alignment checks are needed. For example, where outputs from multiple projects combine into a capability you must stress that the projects will need to frequently collaborate. This is critical at key points in the project lifecycle, such as specification and design. Don't let a project progress beyond these critical points until you are sure all the outputs will fit together as a system. It is a good idea to get the BCMs to help with the scrutiny of such artefacts. If a project cannot be aligned with delivering to the blueprint or the programme objectives then you should be challenging its existence.

Activity	Recommended actions
Control project delivery	You have put in place governance for the programme. While you will normally expect projects to establish their own governance arrangements there are two critical tests you should conduct: ■ Governance in each project must be at least as good as you expect to achieve in the programme. ■ Project arrangements must interface with those in the programme, particularly so that information from the projects is timely, complete and accurate. There are two adages that are worth remembering: ■ Rolled-up rubbish is still rubbish: get the detail right at source. ■ Overall performance is usually no better that the weakest part: programme success is likely to be limited to that of the worst performing project. Risks and issues will keep you very busy. You need to make sure each project is managing risks and issues to an acceptable standard, but you will not normally manage the projects' risks and issues, unless escalated. You will need to take risk and issue information from all projects, from other activities such as benefits realization and from the programme, then make sense of what the total picture tells you. The BCMs need to be heavily involved in approving changes to projects because of the potential business and benefits impact.
Project closure	This is where projects will be handing over their outputs. Unlike in standalone projects this might be initially to the programme. Someone needs to combine outputs from several projects into the system that is the new capability. This must be thoroughly tested before it is allowed to go live. You need to directly take control of this, and you should involve the BCMs as they are your customers. Your attention should then turn to maintaining momentum and focus on securing the improvements and increasing performance, or amending the benefit profiles to reflect capability that will not be available. While this is more the domain of the BCM they will often benefit from your support, as you are likely to have more experience of managing change.

16 Realizing the Benefits

16 Realizing the Benefits

> *'Change is hard because people overestimate the value of what they have and underestimate the value of what they may gain by giving that up.'*
> James Belasco and Ralph Stayer

This is where you prove that all the hard work delivers the dividend. Benefits thinking starts as soon as they are first sketched into the programme brief, but most certainly when the blueprint is agreed, by which time you will have a benefits map and the benefit profiles which will provide the detail. The Realizing the Benefits process formally starts after the approval is given to continue at the end of Defining a Programme, but you should have done a lot of benefits work already by then and be well prepared.

16.1 WHAT DOES MSP HAVE TO SAY?

The purpose of the Realizing the Benefits process is to manage the benefits from their initial identification to their successful realization. The activities cover monitoring the progress of the projects to ensure that the outputs are fit for purpose and can be integrated into operations such that the benefits can be realized.

Realizing the Benefits incorporates the planning and management of the transition from old to new ways of working and the achievement of the outcomes, while ensuring that the operational stability and performance of the operations are maintained. The activities of this process are repeated as necessary for each tranche of the programme.

Three distinct sets of activities are covered here:

- **Manage pre-transition** The analysis, preparation and planning for business transformation
- **Manage transition** Delivering and supporting the changes
- **Manage post-transition** Reviewing progress, measuring performance and adapting to change.

16.1.1 Activities

- Manage pre-transition – the analysis, preparation and planning for business transformation:
  - Establish benefits measurements
  - Monitor benefits realization
  - Plan transition
  - Communicate the change
  - Assess the readiness for change
- Manage transition – delivering and supporting the changes:
  - Initiate transition
  - Establish support arrangements
  - Enact transition
  - Review transition
  - Manage outcome achievement
- Manage post-transition – reviewing progress, measuring performance and adapting to change:
  - Measure benefits
  - Remove access to legacy working practices and systems
  - Respond to changing requirements
  - Monitor and report benefits realization.

16.2 RECOMMENDED ACTIONS

This process is about more than just realizing the actual benefits. It focuses on the change lifecycle and runs throughout the programme lifecycle.

It covers pre-transition, transition and of course post-transition. It is post-transition where the benefits are realized. If the earlier activities are not carried out effectively, then benefits will not be achieved.

While this is more the domain of the BCM, coordination and collaboration with the rest of the programme are critical. This is what you must manage. The recommended actions for the programme manager are shown in Table 16.1.

Hints and tips

This process starts at the beginning of the programme once the programme brief is in place. Do not be fooled into thinking it is something that happens later.

Table 16.1 Recommended actions for the programme manager in Realizing the Benefits

Activity	Recommended actions
Pre-transition	Benefit monitoring is both proactive and reactive. At several critical points in the project lifecycle, such as design, assurance reviews must include the programme view. You need to arrange for someone to explain the emerging outputs and ask BCMs and other operation staff a key question. 'If you receive what you have just seen do you think it will allow you to make sufficient improvements to realize the benefits?' If the answer is 'No', it is for you and the BCMs to fix the problem. You and the BCM are jointly responsible for preparing the transition plan. You are likely to have more planning expertise, and the BCM will be closer to operations. Prior to moving into transition it is really important that there is a baseline measurement of business performance before it starts. You really need to focus on managing risk of business performance degradation or even failure. The programme will be blamed for anything and everything that goes wrong in the coming period, so you need to ensure that you have checked everything, the plans are robust and the contingency plans are tested in case you need to pull out. The BCMs are absolutely critical to this: they know how the business works and they must be completely onside.

Activity	Recommended actions
Manage transition	You need to have made sure all the various elements of the capability are working and their functionality has been signed off by BCMs before you start transition; full sign-off will come later, but you must be confident that this is going to work. You might arrange for temporary operational support to be provided by some people from the projects in the programme, as they have detailed knowledge of the new systems. Some old systems might need decommissioning and an existing project team might be best placed to do this. Some can be decommissioned now. Others are perhaps more appropriately in post-transition when the new systems are fully proven. There will be plenty with their hands up for a better world and some who think they deserve additional features for the pain they have suffered with the new ways of working! In that context, you will need to be providing the filtration system to ensure unreasonable changes to requirements are not being fed into the programme. Some requirements may be better delivered through tactical local changes rather than through projects. When operational people start to use new systems they often discover ways to fine tune them and make them work better. You might want to consider putting these into the design of projects in the next tranche.
Post-transition	The BCMs will be focusing on the performance trends and making doubly sure that the declaration of benefits being achieved is appropriate. It is important that they check the data and, if possible, look for secondary evidence to support not only the short-term achievements but indications that the longer-term direction of travel has been established. Your focus should now be on the next wave of projects and what lessons you can build into them so the next transition is more effective.

17 Closing a Programme

17 Closing a Programme

'Think twice before you speak, because your words and influence will plant the seed of either success or failure in the mind of another.'
Napoleon Hill

There is a temptation to shut the door, turn the lights out and evaporate if things haven't gone too well; however, normally positives will come out of even the worst programmes. Part of the reason that research claims that many benefits are not delivered is because there is a lack of a structured closure to programmes, so the positive effects are not recorded.

If the results of the programme are not objectively measured, people will form their own opinions. Remember most people prefer to spread bad news.

We have simplified the MSP activities so that the guidance is clearer and more specific for your role.

17.1 WHAT DOES MSP HAVE TO SAY?

The purpose of Closing a Programme is to ensure the 'end goal' of formally recognizing that the programme is completed. This is when the programme has delivered the required new capabilities described in the blueprint, and has assessed the outcomes via benefit measures.

17.1.1 Activities

- Confirm that ongoing support is in place
- Confirm programme closure
- Notify people that programme is about to close
- Review programme
- Update and finalize programme information
- Provide feedback to corporate governance
- Disband programme organization and supporting functions.

Hints and tips

Be careful you don't snatch defeat from the jaws of victory. Communicate your successes, even if there aren't many!

17.2 RECOMMENDED ACTIONS

This process covers the structured closure of the programme. Lessons learned and formal handover of documentation and services characterize a successful closure. The recommended actions for the programme manager are shown in Table 17.1.

Table 17.1 Recommended actions for the programme manager in Closing a Programme

Activity	Recommended actions
Prepare to close	Your checklist at this point is: ■ All the capabilities in the blueprint are operational ■ Outcomes for all the capabilities can be observed ■ The business case has been satisfied in that the actual time, cost and benefits are recorded in the final version ■ Benefits are self-sustaining ■ Last tranche has been completed as per the programme plan ■ No risks or issues are outstanding. You will need to focus on how the momentum for change is going to be sustained when the new services are passed into the operational environment. Where new services or supply arrangements have been put into place, it is essential that there is a planned and structured handover of contracts and contract management arrangements to your business areas. In-house support, help desks etc. will now be totally responsible for handling incidents.
Close	This is where you can enhance or damage your career. You are now going to communicate closure and therefore what the programme has achieved. Make sure this is clear. Premature closure does not mean you have failed, providing that this is not due to your poor management. If the programme is closing prematurely it is in your interests to explain clearly the reasons why and what has been achieved and learned.
Disband the team	Not everyone will still be active in the programme at this point. But it is good to reward all those who have worked to make the changes happen. This does not have to be financial reward, though that is nice if possible: a thank you, maybe a few beers or similar can go a long way. Also make sure that everyone's staff record is updated to show their personal achievements. You might need to work with some of these people again so it is good to part on best terms.

Appendix A: Information summary

Appendix A: Information summary

Programmes generate lots of information and it can be difficult to work out how to link it all together.

The information can be grouped into 'baselines', which are sets of information that are related to one another. Table A.1 shows the information baselines from MSP.

Table A.1 Information baselines

Information baseline	Summary	Documents
Boundary	Information that sets out the direction and scope of the programme and as such is the first information set to be created.	Benefit profile Benefits map Blueprint Business case Programme brief Programme definition document Programme mandate Projects dossier Vision statement
Governance	Information that sets out the standards and frameworks within which the programme will be delivered; it defines 'how' the programme will be managed. The areas that need to be covered are in the strategies. These will not change unless they don't work or the context for the programme changes.	Benefits management strategy Information management strategy Issue management strategy Monitoring and control strategy Organization structure Quality and assurance strategy Resource management strategy Risk management strategy Stakeholder engagement strategy

Table continues

Table A.1 *continued*

Information baseline	Summary	Documents
Management	Information that is created and used to manage the delivery of the programme; it defines 'what' activities will be undertaken by 'whom' to deliver the programme. The information in these documents may be changing on a daily basis so the baseline is more difficult to maintain and may need to be updated regularly (e.g. quarterly) but it does need to remain under control.	Benefits realization plan Information management plan Issue register Programme communications plan Programme preparation plan Programme plan Quality and assurance plan Resource management plan Risk register Stakeholder profiles

Index

Index

Bold page numbers indicate figures,
italic numbers indicate tables.